SANDWICH'D

SANDWICH'D

MY LIFE
BETWEEN THE BREADS

Peter Roseman

Illustrated by Melanie B. Wong

PLUM BAY PUBLISHING, LLC

Library of Congress Control Number: 2018954998
ISBN: 978-0-9988617-6-0
Printed in the United States of America

Book jacket design by Lauren Harvey
Edited by Jeremy Townsend
Interior text design by Barbara Aronica-Buck

DEDICATED TO MY WIFE, MEI,
AND DAUGHTER, LILLIAN,
WHO COMPLETE THE SANDWICH OF MY LIFE!

CONTENTS

INTRODUCTION

I LOVE LUNCH. I always have. Specifically, I love sandwiches—the fresh breads, the assorted fillings and the multitudinous types of condiments, and so many combinations from which to choose. Whoever thought combining sliced turkey breast, coleslaw, cheddar cheese, and Russian dressing on a poppy seed roll would taste so good? How about a really good meatball Parmesan hero with just the right amount of tomato sauce and melted mozzarella cheese that stretches when you pull the sandwich apart. Just thinking about it makes me hungry. From my earliest memories, I recall watching my mom prepare a peanut butter and jelly sandwich with just the right amount of each spread on two slices of fresh white bread. Add a bag of chips and a glass of milk, and I was in sandwich heaven. I would gobble down the first half of the sandwich, then slowly savor the second half until I'd eaten every last crumb. As I got older, my love affair with lunch and the sandwich continued. I became a bit of a sandwich connoisseur, indulging in chicken Parmesan heroes, Italian combos, and rare roast beef on a kaiser with lettuce, tomatoes and mayo. These classics, as well as numerous others, became staples of my diet. I began to frequent local sandwich shops and chose my favorites in town. One might have the best roast beef, whereas another might have made the tastiest egg salad in Westchester County. It never occurred to me that someday I would own and operate my own sandwich shop, making and eating sandwiches every day. But that is exactly what happened.

Sandwiches are my passion.

Some people are landscapers, others work in construction, or in offices, or in any number of occupations. I make sandwiches. I feed all of those people: the landscapers, the office workers, the construction workers, and people from dozens more vocations who all buy sandwiches from my shop. Along with my family, I have owned and operated a sandwich shop, Gourmet Galley, in lower Fairfield County, Connecticut, since March 1993. We've been making sandwiches for hungry customers on lunch break day after day since then. We've sent out countless sandwich trays to corporations, big and small. Since I was twenty-three, just about every day, including weekends, has been spent operating the shop. I've watched the weeks turn into years and the years pile up like turkey on a mile-high club sandwich. Long days have been filled with ups and downs, some typical, some not so much. Employees, vendors, and customers have all played an important role in this journey. The one constant, the sandwich, has been the main ingredient in my life. I've been creating, selling, and eating sandwiches for a very long time. Along with my experience as a teen, I've been "sandwich'd" in the food service life for over thirty years.

When my mom, dad, and I decided to invest in a sandwich shop we thought it would be relatively easy. We actually thought the business would allow us to take afternoons off occasionally and even take regular vacations. Our dependable, well-trained staff could handle it in our absence. We were soooo naïve! What could possibly go wrong? What could possibly happen? A lot, actually—enough to fill a book, or maybe two. (Let's see how this one does!) We never thought our one sandwich shop would become a 24/7/365-day lifetime commitment, but that's exactly what happened.

For this book, I've chosen 19 recipes to highlight, 19 sandwiches with 19 stories, all with one thing in common: each tasty sandwich relates to its accompanying story.

The recipes I've chosen include some old favorites and some Gourmet Galley classics. There are also a few international delights I never knew existed before I owned a sandwich shop. Every recipe is delicious. Trust me. I've prepared, eaten, and sold every one of them. The sandwich ingredients are easy to gather and put together with no need for long prep times. With the exception of the Cuban, the sandwiches should mostly take 30 minutes or less to prepare. Each recipe yields four sandwiches, along with the ingredients and instructions, which are more like guidelines, subject to personal preference. One thing I've learned over the years; sandwich combinations can, and will, change, sometimes drastically, according to taste. I've actually encountered people who prefer sandwiches with no condiments! There are no glazes, sauces or pretentious demi-glaces. Easy to prepare, the sandwiches are stomach fillin' and hunger killin' creations perfect for lunch or any informal gathering. My wife suggested I include a chip selection with each recipe because, without a doubt, chips are the best accompaniment to a great sandwich. The illustrations accompanying the recipes add to the pure essence of each sandwich. Pay close attention to the details.

Before another page is turned, a warning: This book may cause yearning, craving, or increased appetite that may well lead to ravenous gluttony. When reading, if you begin to feel hungry, stop and immediately make yourself a sandwich. Enjoy!!

SANDWICH'D

TOO FEW PEOPLE UNDERSTAND
A REALLY GOOD SANDWICH.

—JAMES BEARD

CHAPTER 1

SANDWICHES RULE

When I was about twenty years old, during the summer between my freshman and sophomore years at college, I worked for a maintenance company located in New York City. I cleaned, delivered mail, and ran a freight elevator. This was the only job I ever held that was not in food service and I did enjoy it. There are times, on especially difficult days in the shop, when I look back on that job and second-guess my decision to enter food service. Being from the suburbs, in Chappaqua, New York, I'd never commuted to a job before and had little experience with public transportation. This inexperience led to the first "Aha!" moment of my life.

On my first day of scheduled work, I managed to find my way to the main office of the company that would be employing me for the next eight weeks. I was given instructions from an older man behind a desk. We were separated by a thick glass partition. He told me where to report for work. He sounded as if he'd been smoking all his life. He had a deep, hoarse voice that emanated from behind the glass. He was a little intimidating. His speech was monosyllabic, and I bet he forgot about me as soon as I walked away.

I scribbled down the address and thanked him. Off I went down the elevator and onto the mean streets of New York City. When my feet hit the pavement, I was completely stumped. I looked at my paper and then looked around. All I could see were traffic lights, street signs, and a sea of people, all in an incredible hurry. I figured they were heading to work, like me, but I noticed something interesting about their demeanors:

very few of them were smiling. Most of these pedestrians shared a grim look of determination. Their expressions reflected the truth that, whether they liked it or not, they had to go to work.

At this point I did the only logical thing: I called my sister, Leslie, a veteran of New York City life. When I told her my destination she directed me to the subway that would take me there. On the subway platform there were more determined-looking people ready to cram themselves into the subway cars that kept whizzing by. I wondered to myself if anyone who went to work was happy. Finally, I caught the correct train and reached my destination, a place called the South Ferry station. Once off the subway, I looked across the street and, lo and behold, there stood the building I was instructed to find. It was a nondescript, five-story building that was completely vacant. Its offices were empty, and its floors were bare. The only thing that remained were dozens of file cabinets on every floor. The supervisor on the job, a stocky man with a toothless smile and a mouth like a sewer, was busy cleaning the cabinets when I arrived. "Come back tomorra" he said, "we don't fuckin' need ya 'til tomorra." The next day I would be working next to the supervisor, along with a handful more workers, scrubbing cabinets in an empty building. I happily complied and headed out the door. This work thing was great so far! I'd explored a new world, learned to ride the subway, and so far didn't have to lift a finger for work. And I got paid. Summer was off to a great start! The next thing that happened to me would change the trajectory of my life in a way I never imagined.

With most of the morning behind me I was left in the city with nothing to do. I decided to find a shady tree and plan the remainder of the day. There was a line of trees running along the sidewalk. The trees ran parallel to a very tall building, at least twenty stories high. The sun beamed down, lighting up the entryway so I could clearly see the revolving doors. It must have been around 11:30. It was at that very moment that I noticed a change. Men and women began pouring out of the building. Pairs, groups, and individuals exiting the building welcomed by a beautiful, sunny spring day. If I had to guess, they were mostly lawyers, stockbrokers and executive assistants. It was as if a huge spotlight had landed on everyone. They were smiling, laughing, chatting, and enjoying themselves. Gone was that look of grim determination I'd noticed earlier. This was more like it. I had to figure out what caused this change in demeanor. In about ten minutes I had my answer. The men and women began returning with bags in their hands. It was lunchtime. I watched as some reentered the building while others remained outside. Those outside sat with friends or colleagues and began to eat. Some were eating pizza or Chinese food. Most, however, were eating sandwiches. They were enjoying big, tasty, overstuffed sandwiches bursting with ingredients, flavors, and aromas that made my stomach grumble and my mouth water. I noticed sandwiches on rolls, heroes, and pitas. When I saw a man engulfing a gyro dripping with tzatziki sauce, it brought me back to the first time I ate one of those. Oh the memories! I noted the sandwich eaters ate with the most gusto and had the biggest smiles. This was my "Aha!" moment. I realized right then that lunch was the most important and celebrated part of the workday, and the star of the celebration was my favorite food, the sandwich. After a few moments, armed with my newest realization, I headed to the nearest deli for a roast beef sandwich. Roast beef on a kaiser with lettuce, tomatoes, and mayo—one of my faves at the time, with chips and a soda, hit the spot. After lunch I headed home.

I spent the whole summer in New York City that year. The job had taken me to a permanent location in mid-town. For eight weeks I became one of those determined-looking people, getting to work in the morning. By lunchtime though, with a few of my work friends, the day always took a turn for the better. We scoured the area for the best sandwiches. On the menu that summer were meatball subs, Italian combos, turkey, roast beef, and tuna salad. I remember watching the sandwich makers behind the deli counter as they juggled dozens of orders put in front of them by order takers. There was a certain intoxicating energy in these busy sandwich shops. Members of the staff worked in unison as the phone rang incessantly and the line of people always seemed to get longer. I was amazed that they kept things straight. I remember wondering, for a second or two, if I could do that job? I wondered if I could be the one handing the workers their lunchtime sandwich and improving their day.

There was a courtyard on the side of our building where, weather permitting, my colleagues and I sat and ate. Just like the people I watched my first day in the city, everything was on hold as we ate lunch. It was a time to celebrate the middle of the workday. I loved the anticipation of slowly removing the sandwich out of the bag and unwrapping it. A quick inspection, a few nibbles to tantalize the taste buds, then total satisfaction bite after bite. Along with a cold drink and a bag of chips, this was lunch done right. There was an old security guard who walked around the courtyard checking brown bags for bottles and cans. Apparently, alcohol was strictly prohibited in the courtyard. I always thought he was checking out what everyone was eating for lunch. Was he a sandwich lover, searching for good lunch ideas? That summer was a learning experience for me. The lesson I learned between 12 and 1 p.m., lunch hour, would stay with me forever. The most important part of any workday is lunch, and nothing beats a good sandwich.

CHAPTER 2
"YOU KNOW NOTHING ABOUT FOOD!"

Lehigh

One day toward the end of my illustrious college career, probably while on spring break, Mom, Dad, and I began having a conversation. Soon I would graduate and, up to that point, my main accomplishments at school amounted to taking long afternoon naps and drinking copious amounts of alcohol. I also smoked plenty of weed and might have experimented with psychedelics on occasion. I called it "higher" education at the time. That could even explain the long naps! My less-than-proud parents were concerned, rightfully so, about my plans for the future. Problem was, I didn't really have any plans. To make matters worse, I majored in English.

So we sat and brainstormed for a while. We decided it might be wise to search for a small business. The three of us got along well and figured, if we put our minds together, perhaps we could find something suitable that we could all do. My dad was at the tail end of a career on Wall Street and was searching for something new. My mom also showed an interest in working, if the situation was right. Different business options came to mind including a grocery store, a produce market, and even a pet store. At one point, Mom suggested the food/catering business. I had restaurant jobs over the years and always liked the work, so it seemed logical. By that time, I had worked in a pizzeria, a busy seafood restaurant on the Hudson River, and even a country club restaurant among others. Once, a friend and I even opened our own snack bar at our high school's summer session. It took place in the home economics room. We didn't make much money, but we had fun fooling around with girls all summer. This experience taught me a few things about being self-employed. I balanced the books, stocked the fridge and learned the value of customer service. Despite all of this, Dad looked at the two of us and said something that will go down in the annals of famous family quotations: "Why a food business? You know nothing about food!"

The conversation might have ended there but nobody had any better ideas, so it was decided, despite our aforementioned shortcomings, we'd look for a food/catering business. After a short search we found a spot. It seemed a bit complicated—sandwiches, catering, and small meat market/grocery, but we decided to go for it. We bought the small Italian market, located in Hamden, Connecticut, in 1991, from a man who had run it for years. Not long after we got there, it was clear that the marriage was anything but smooth. We were inexperienced, and it showed. The three of us attempted to learn the business as fast as possible. Our favorite parts were the busy lunch line and the catering. The sandwich line sometimes ran twenty-people deep. The adrenaline burst started around 11 a.m. and began to fade around 1:30 p.m. or so when the line began to slow down. It was a challenge every day to send happy customers on lunch break out the door with a great sandwich in their hands. Learning how to work the sandwich line at lunch would provide valuable experience for the years to come. The catering aspect was one of our strengths as well, especially with the few corporate clients in the area. Clients called us for lunches, sandwich trays, salads, and drinks for meetings at noon. Preparing these lunches would become one of our signature services in the future, and our speed and turnaround became legendary. Unfortunately, the meat market proved to be too much for us beginners to handle. With obstacles mounting and bills piling up, after about two years, we decided to sell the business. It was the best decision we ever made.

Soon after selling our first small business we got a call from a broker who had a real sandwich shop available in Greenwich. It was called Gourmet Galley and it specialized in sandwiches and corporate catering—almost too good to be true. Undeterred by our first experience, we decided to check it out. Between us, Mom, Dad, and I had multiple college degrees so we figured, in the right situation, we could operate a successful small business. The shop had great visibility, right on the main street, Greenwich Avenue, in town. The building was number 100, right across the street from a busy CVS pharmacy. After a bit of due diligence, including several menu samplings, we figured we'd give the food industry one more go. It was the first time, but not the last, that I tried curried mayo—excellent with turkey breast, lettuce and tomatoes in a pita! The tuna salad was fantastic, and the fresh turkey was the real thing, off the bone. There was a "secret" ingredient in the tuna, which we've kept secret as well (although you might find it hidden somewhere within the pages of this book!). It was the perfect business for us, so we bought it.

My family has now been operating Gourmet Galley ever since we turned the key in late March of 1993. At the time of purchase, the shop was struggling and in the throes of a downturn. The economic conditions didn't help either, so Mom, Dad, and I used every ounce of our energy to learn the trade and improve our new sandwich shop. Seven-day work weeks were typical. Dinner time was dominated by conversations about the shop. How could we improve it? How could we get more customers? How could we make more sandwiches? It was a twenty-four-hour-a-day obsession, and it paid off. In a matter of months, we'd made huge strides with walk-in customers as well as corporate clients. It was a major change from our first experience and quite a relief. In a few years, we boasted a corporate client list that was easily in the hundreds. Month-end billing was an affair that took several days to complete. Our sales numbers continued to rise year after year and the sandwich line got longer and longer.

Dad skillfully worked the books and helped out at lunch, begrudgingly. Side by side, Mom and I made sandwiches and handled the operations. As the business grew, extra staff was hired. Lunch rush sometimes began at around 9 a.m., or earlier, and didn't finish until after two. Clients ordered sandwich trays daily, walk-in traffic increased dramatically, and lunch delivery became a way of life. There were mornings when we began making sandwiches at 7:30! Companies began sending large lunch orders in by 9 a.m. with long lists of sandwiches, soups, and salads to be prepared and delivered by noon. There were days when lunch was so busy that we had four, five, or six people making deliveries. The phone rang constantly, reminding me of the sandwich shops I went to in the city when I was a working stiff. Now I was the one juggling orders and making sandwiches—though, no matter how busy, I always made time to eat a sandwich for lunch. Vendors delivered fresh produce, sandwich meats, dry goods and paper supplies on a daily basis. Customers eagerly awaited our daily special menus, which were faxed first thing in the morning. It was sandwiches, sandwiches and more sandwiches. The kitchen was small, but we made the most of every inch of space. There was even a slow-cook turkey oven in one corner that ran twenty-four hours a day. This was the golden era for Gourmet Galley. As in life, things would change.

Landlords have a history of getting what they want. In our case, landlords, for a variety of reasons, have wanted us to move. Being forced to move is no easy task for any business, much less a sandwich shop or restaurant. There's major planning involved. The store must be moved and put into place at another suitable location without disrupting day-to-day operations. There's a risk of lost customers, and finding appropriate workspace is challenging. In our case we were forced to invest in preexisting food service operations rather than building a shop from the ground up, which could potentially take a year or more. This happened to us not once, not twice, but three times. Gourmet Galley moved once in 2000, again in 2003, and last in 2008. In the second and third locations we found ourselves struggling for the first time. I consider them our lean years. Our locations were off the beaten path, and maintaining clients became much more difficult. Competition had begun to sprout up all over town in the early part of the century. Despite the ups and downs, through the first eight years of the twenty-first century, we continued to make the Gourmet Galley the best place in town to get a sandwich. In 2008, we found the location at which we reside to this day. We moved from Greenwich to Stamford, a few exits north, a small spot perfect for our operation at 469 Fairfield Avenue. This address would provide us with a workable mix of corporate, industrial, and blue-collar clients. Since our move, we have maintained an excellent walk-in trade, serviced corporate clients seamlessly, and found a space we can happily call home. Hopefully, we'll never have to move again. I'm getting way too old for that. Sometimes we laugh about that day so long ago when Dad made his comment. It's been over twenty-five years, and by now we know plenty about food, especially sandwiches.

CHAPTER 3
SANDWICHES NEAR AND FAR

Aside from taste, there are two great things about sandwiches: convenience and accessibility. Sandwich shops are easily found on nearly every corner in some cities and towns. That means that pretty much wherever you are, if so desired, you can find a good sandwich. Trust me on this one. I've even found excellent sandwiches in Iceland. Of course, close to home, you should have a favorite sandwich shop. It might be the nearest local deli or market where you head when it's time for lunch. If it's a good one, they should recognize you and greet you accordingly. If you eat the same sandwich day after day, week after week, they should know that as well. It's invaluable to have a good relationship with your sandwich shop. It can be the difference between a great lunch hour and a lunch hour that leaves you dreading the afternoon. Another thing to look for at your local shop is a good "Daily Specials" menu. Unlike restaurants, who might use leftovers as specials, good sandwich shops will have daily bread deliveries and most ingredients are sliced fresh daily. Our "Daily Special" menu is always headlined by a tasty sandwich.

While traveling, eating sandwiches should be an indulgence. The simple sandwich rule while on the road is easy: experiment. Try the local fare. Certain cities have become famously known for their sandwiches. Philadelphia has the cheesesteak; Boston, the lobster roll; New Orleans, the Po'Boy. You get the idea. Do yourself a favor and, upon arrival to a new city, ask the nearest local what's good to eat. Where can I get the best this place has to offer? Many times, it will be a sandwich. Go get that sandwich. Make it your first meal, and, if it's as good as advertised, your last meal and perhaps one or two meals in between before leaving that city.

Long lines should never deter you from getting into a local favorite. While in Iceland to run a marathon one summer, my wife and I noticed a very long line. It led to a hot dog stand. (Yes, I consider hot dogs and hamburgers to be sandwiches.) "How good could they possibly be?" I recall asking my wife, so we skipped it. A few years later I was watching a food show, and there it was, ranked as one of the best hot dog stands in the world: the Iceland Dog. I wanted to hop a plane right then and rectify the error of my ways. In fact, my wife and I have discussed returning there just for the hot dog. I consider passing on that hot dog stand one of my biggest culinary gaffes. Heed my story and don't make the same mistake! Even if the line seems long, it's usually worth the wait. You can return home and cross another one off your sandwich bucket list. When you hear someone say, "I traveled to XYZ City last week and had amazing sandwich," smile to yourself. Been there, eaten that!

I've learned that wherever you go, sandwiches are a local favorite. Cities all over the world put their own special spin on them that make the eating experience unique and worth the trip. Once, while in San Francisco to run another marathon, I was killing time the day before the race. I found a local sandwich shop and noticed a particular loaf of bread behind the counter. It looked like a seven grain but not like any I'd seen on the east coast. I grabbed my spot in line and ordered a turkey club sandwich, pointing to the bread I'd seen. The girl behind the counter looked at me, then at the clock, then at my running shoes, and made me the sandwich. It was 7:30 a.m. The sandwich was so good I made a note to return after the race. Sure enough, after 26.2 miles the following day, a few bottles of sports drink and a doughnut or two, I headed back to the shop for another. I finished the sandwich while heading to the airport. I've spent the last twelve years searching for that bread. It was that good. When I eat out, either locally or abroad, indulging in sandwiches will always be at the top of my list of best things to do for lunch.

CHAPTER 4
SANDWICHES AT HOME

There's nothing better than spending quality time at home with family or friends sharing laughter, good times, and enjoying fresh homemade sandwiches for lunch, especially weekends.

As Saturday morning slowly becomes Saturday afternoon, hunger sets in, and it's time for lunch. Very little prep time is needed to create the perfect lunchtime meal. But there are certain items every kitchen should have stocked to ensure complete sandwich satisfaction. Below is a checklist of sandwich necessities:

BREAD   When eating sandwiches at home, *always* have fresh bread around. There's no excuse for anything else. I like to have a few different kinds so there's a little selection. Your bread does not have to be fancy; most grocery stores offer a wide selection of sliced breads and rolls. However, if it's the weekend and you want lunch to be a little special, go to the bakery for some fresh-out-of-the-oven bread. There are so many flavors nowadays. At work, we get a pesto bread that is out-of-this-world good. Even if you don't finish it, you can always toast it up in the morning for breakfast.

COLD CUTS   By any other name, top quality lunch meat and cheeses are absolutely a household requirement. Make sure you buy products from a busy market to ensure the meat is fresh. If you enter one of those markets that has a few sad pieces of ham and some olive loaf staring at you with a single stack of yellowish-white American cheese, chances are they don't make too many sandwiches or sell too many cold cuts. When fresh, meats and cheeses last for several days in the fridge, so buy according to your lunchtime plans. Although it's not really a cold cut, don't forget the bacon! Also, buy a reputable brand of cold cuts. It's worth the cost. You can always ask the deli man for a taste. You will be much happier in the long run. Some less expensive cold cuts use fillers and have minimal flavor. Last, experiment with a variety of flavors. We offer about six types of turkey at a given time. Try a spiced ham or honey turkey, or even a pepper jack cheese. Your taste buds will thank you.

LEFTOVERS Leftovers from last night's dinner can make an exceptional lunch. Maybe you had spaghetti and meatballs. Meatball wedges make great sandwiches. Brisket or roast beef leftovers are perfect in a sandwich with a crusty roll and some homemade Thousand Island dressing (ketchup, mayo and sweet relish). The leftover turkey from Thanksgiving makes great turkey salad with some chopped celery, salt, pepper, and, of course, mayonnaise. You may even want to plan dinner with the next day's lunch in mind. What can I make for a meal that will become a great lunch sandwich tomorrow? So many options, so don't throw anything away.

CANS, JARS & CONDIMENTS The first rule of any household is always to have some canned tuna around. Tuna salad is synonymous with sandwiches and lunchtime. It's easy to make and tastes great. It can be very healthy too, depending on how it's made. As for condiments, the list is long. Mayonnaise and mustard are a good start. The mayo should be limited to brand names only (you *can* taste the difference). Mayo is to the sandwich maker what tomato sauce is to the Italian cook. It makes everything taste better! Mustards are another story. No longer are we a one- or two-mustard world. Specialty stores have dozens of mustards to choose from. Honey, coarse, yellow, spicy, just to name a few, are excellent additions to any sandwich. For other condiments, it's a matter of taste. Horseradish, pickle chips or slices, jalapeños, banana peppers, roasted red peppers, and olives are all readily available at any grocery store and make a good sandwich great! The two most important jars to have in the house are one of peanut butter and one jelly. No house is a sandwich home without these two essentials. By the way, when making a PBJ using only one knife, always spread the peanut first, then the jelly. Keeping a jar of jelly with traces of peanut butter is okay, but a jar of peanut butter with traces of jelly is simply uncivilized! Also, if you have kids around, and they have been a little lethargic lately, a jar of the marshmallow spread will get them going in no time. Make sure to keep a good stock of cans, jars and condiments in the house. They usually have long expiration dates and you just never know what you might want to add to spice up your lunch.

VEGGIES Other than vegetarian sandwiches, the sandwich had never been known for vegetables. That has changed over the years. Lettuce and tomatoes should always be readily available. Cucumbers, sliced thin, make a great addition to any sandwich as well. Carrots and celery are essential, especially for tuna or chicken salad. Also, a touch of red onion on any sandwich is perfect as long as you don't have an important meeting in the afternoon. If you like coleslaw on your sandwich, or on the side, keep a head of cabbage around. It lasts a long time, and homemade coleslaw is so much better than store bought. Find a good recipe: one with mayo, sour cream, and heavy cream makes unforgettable coleslaw. Last, don't forget avocado, the ultimate sandwich topper. It's come a long way in the past twenty years from when it was used only in Mexican food. Avocados ripen in a few days and make any sandwich top notch.

CHIPS I could probably write an entire book on the chip industry, and maybe I will someday. Chips just go with sandwiches, plain and simple. There are so many flavors, brands, shapes, sizes, etc., it would be unfair to say one is superior. It's just something about this salty snack that goes so well with the sandwich that you must have a bag or two on hand at all times. Skip the low-fat and fat-free types. Go for the hard stuff. Also, try different kinds. The chip companies have been so thoughtful to present us with a wide variety; give'em all a try.

There are plenty of other ingredients available for creating the perfect sandwich, but if you start with the list above, lunch is set for quite a while. Hummus, for example, has gained popularity as a sandwich spread and is excellent, available in a wide variety of flavors.

Now that you are well stocked, it's time to create. As you enter the kitchen and begin the sandwich preparation, take a good look around. First, consider how many sandwiches are to be made. Let's say a few people are coming over for lunch. The semolina heroes picked up this morning should be perfect. Never, ever leave a bakery without semolina heroes if they are fresh. There's something about that semolina flour and the sesame seeds on top that make it the "hero" of the bread box. If you are not in the mood, the aroma of fresh semolina will put you in the mood for a sandwich. Place your heroes on the counter along with ingredients from the fridge. The main rule to remember about sandwiches at home is to trust your taste buds. If the combo tastes good to you, chances are everyone will enjoy it.

Carefully study the veggies. Notice the pure redness of the tomatoes, and the crispy lettuce. The avocados, if ripe, will be soft to the touch. Open a jar of pickle chips and let the aroma fill your nostrils with the smell of pure satisfaction. Choose your condiments carefully. A spicy mustard and mayo combo might be the best marriage in the sandwich world. As you open the package of freshly sliced turkey, take a small taste and let the flavor fill your mouth. The pepper jack cheese will perfectly enhance the sandwiches. These are going to be some *gooood* sandwiches. You are now ready to start.

With a serrated knife, slowly slice the semolina heroes lengthwise to expose the middle of the bread. The fresh bread should be soft in the middle and crisp on the outside. Take a butter knife and spread the condiments. Mayo on one side and mustard on the other. Cover the bread completely. Now begin to layer, first the lettuce and tomatoes. As a side note, if you plan on using an oil-and-vinegar-based dressing, squirt it directly on lettuce. The lettuce will hold it in place. Vinaigrettes will roll off the tomatoes and, if put on bread first, will make the sandwich too soggy. (By the way, combining mayo, mustard, and vinaigrette on one sandwich is a taste like no other, like a condiment vortex to be entered into carefully but with serious gusto! It's a combination not to be attempted by the meek or timid.)

After placing the tomatoes, add the pickle chips and sliced avocados. The sandwiches are now ready for the main ingredient. Layer sliced turkey so it covers the entire sandwich end to end. The last thing you want is the last bite or two to be plain bread. Make sure each sandwich has enough meat; there's no reason to hold back now. Last, add the sliced cheese. Before closing the sandwiches with the top of the semolina, check to make sure they look good. Is there enough meat? Should you add some onion? If everything is in order, close the sandwiches and cut in halves, thirds or quarters depending on the size of the bread. Before you place the sandwiches on plates for your guests, take one last look. If the sight makes your mouth water, they were made correctly. You might even want to send a picture to your friends! Nobody should miss this sandwich. Grab some fresh bags of chips from the cupboard. You and your fellow hungry diners are about to obtain sandwich satisfaction. The sandwich done right . . . at home.

CHAPTER 5

NEVER EAT IN A DARK RESTAURANT

When I was young, Sundays were special. My family, all incredibly rigid about our schedules, still managed to have a meal together. There was Sunday at temple; soccer games, and jobs during the day; but Sunday night we went out for dinner. In today's world it seems almost prehistoric to think that a family would only dine out once a week, but that's how it was. Before going out, there was the obligatory discussion, or argument, as to where we would break bread. One of us preferred the burger joint while another wanted pizza. This fight usually concluded with one of us children sulking in one corner while the others rejoiced at getting their way. Sure, there were three children, but majority rule had not quite made it into our vernacular. Most of the time, the winner was the child who was loudest. And off we went.

One meal we all liked was Chinese food. Everyone could find something they liked on the menu, and, if worse came to worse, we could stuff ourselves with those crunchy noodles that are set on each table before the meal. They were especially good dipped in duck sauce. Chinese restaurants were scarce in our section of Westchester County, but down the road, in the next town over, Mt. Kisco, we all agreed the restaurant on the corner was the best. I remember it was kind of spooky going in there because the lights were very dim. There was a flight of stairs that led down to the open dining room. The stairway had lights just like in movie theaters, and we half expected the host to carry a flashlight. Upon being seated, we were surrounded by other diners whose faces were

18

difficult to make out due to the darkness. A great place to take your mistress, perhaps. Despite the darkness, the food was good. We never questioned the dim lights. We just assumed that customers liked it that way. My mom and I used to order an item called a Pu-Pu Platter. Being a little boy, I thought the name was funny, but it was cool because the food came with a tiny "grill" where you could re-cook the already cooked ribs and chicken. We could also count on good soup, lo-mein, and other standard Chinese menu items. All in all, the whole family enjoyed eating there and we were a little surprised and disappointed a few years later when they closed their doors.

Fast forward about twenty years. Mom, Dad, and I had learned early on that the responsibilities of a small-business owner are endless. Cooking, cleaning, and maintaining staff were part of a long list of never-ending tasks to keep our business moving forward. We learned something new every day, enjoyed the work, and thrived at our location in Greenwich. Some things, like customer service, were obvious, while others were works in progress. One such issue was extermination. It is extremely important, we learned, to maintain a schedule of extermination maintenance. Keeping a food service establishment pest free is imperative to its success. We learned early to dispose of cardboard boxes because pests often bred in the glue. Also, we were told to stuff any wall holes with steel wool and to reinforce them with a layer of plywood; believe it or not, that method keeps pests out. We learned to do anything to keep the food safe from unwanted guests. The man who taught us was named Doug, exterminator to the stars.

Doug was quite a character, an old-timer in the business who knew all the tricks and liked to talk about them. On his monthly trips to our establishment, he loved to regale us with tales of chasing mice or scaring carpenter ants. Doug used to drop names of famous people whose homes he'd been servicing for years. He wasn't supposed to give out addresses but sometimes he'd slip one in. We'd listen to him, not sure if he was fabricating everything. His co-workers used to make fun of him. "He does more talking than exterminating," they'd say. He may not have been the best in the business, but he was the most amusing. One day I asked him a question. I wanted him to describe the worst restaurant he'd ever serviced, the place with the most pests, and what the job entailed. Without hesitation Doug went into a description of a dark Chinese restaurant in Mt. Kisco, New York. My mouth dropped, and my eyes opened wide, as the tale of this restaurant unfolded. He described how his crew would feel their way into the dark dining room and kitchen. After covering all cooking equipment and food, with masks covering their faces, he and his team would spray a dense fog of chemicals around the entire restaurant. They would then head outside and return after thirty minutes. Presumably, this gave the chemicals time to take effect, since the idea was to exterminate pests, not themselves! Upon re-entering the restaurant, they would turn on the lights. Armed with shovels, rakes and other serious tools of the trade, along with fifty-five-gallon trash bags and extra-thick latex gloves, the crew would proceed to scoop, shovel, sweep and otherwise dispose of dead pests, feces, and anything else your imagination could conjure up. The worst extermination job by far, Doug said. His crew dreaded the schedule when it was time to head over to the Chinese restaurant. He recalled they began talking about the dirty job several days in advance. Some of the crew members would begin to perspire as they visualized the day when they had to re-enter this restaurant of horrors. It was that unpleasant.

When he'd finished the story, I insisted on asking the name of the place, just to be sure. He hesitated, and then told me it didn't really matter because it had closed years ago. I said the name of the place at which my family dined many years ago. His look said it all. It was, of course, my family's favorite Chinese restaurant. After the initial shock dissipated I just shrugged it off. It was no wonder those lights were so dim. Gives a whole new meaning to the words Pu-Pu Platter, though.

BAHN MI'

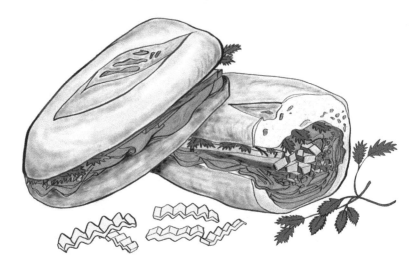

There are many variations of this Vietnamese Classic. The chips can be found at any Asian specialty grocery store.

INGREDIENTS

4 pc thinly sliced pork cutlet lightly seasoned with salt, pepper, and minced garlic

4 6-inch heroes

1 cup shredded daikon

1 cup shredded carrots

1 cucumber, thinly sliced

½ cup chopped cilantro

1 sliced fresh jalapeño

½ cup real mayonnaise

1 T hot sauce

½ cup water

½ cup rice vinegar

½ cup granulated sugar

INSTRUCTIONS

Whisk water, vinegar, and sugar in a bowl until sugar is dissolved. Add daikon and carrots. Let sit for several hours to pickle.

Set broiler on 400 degrees and cook pork cutlets until they reach an interior temperature of 155 degrees, 5–10 minutes. Let cool. When cool, thinly slice and put aside.

In mixing bowl combine mayo and hot sauce to form sandwich spread.

Slice open 6-inch heroes so they lay flat on table. Spread each side with mayo mixture. On bottom half of bread layer sliced pork cutlets. Place pickled veggies on top of pork followed by a layer of thinly sliced cucumbers. Top off with chopped cilantro and sliced jalapeños. Cover each with top half of bread and cut each sandwich in half.

Plate and serve with shrimp chips (found in Asian markets).

CHAPTER 6
MY FIRST TIME

When I was about fifteen, summer was the time to explore. I'd grown out of camp and needed to find a new adventure. Staying home was not an option so, along with a friend, I decided to go on a group bike tour of New England. The trip was a three- to four-week journey on bike through the mountains of Vermont and the hills of New Hampshire, including a short canoe trip through part of Maine. We biked during the day, stopping for meals and sights, and then camped out at night either on the side of the road, or at campsites. The group consisted mostly of boys, but there were a few girls. Our two leaders, Judy and Craig, were employees of the touring company, and were both in their twenties.

All in all, it was a challenging and fun experience. I still remember the pain of riding up a thirteen-mile mountain, and the exhilaration of zooming down the backside at breakneck speed. I also remember the nights around the campfire sharing stories. The girls would read Tarot cards and the boys would entertain each other with tales of conquest back home, embellished I'm sure. S'mores at night and cereal eaten out of the small cardboard box in the morning reminded us we were indeed in the great outdoors. There was plenty of laughter to go around and, though it was only a short time, the group became close. It was quite a coming-of-age experience for me, in more ways than one. I would return from this bike tour a changed teenager.

Judy was an excellent rider with muscular legs and defined upper body, the result of miles and miles on the bike. She was always in control and the tour followed her lead, even when she insisted on stopping at a garage sale to buy a pair of jeans, for a quarter if I recall. You can't imagine the bargains to be had at tag sales in that part of the country. Craig was a different story. He was a decent rider, but was much happier staying at the back, taking his time. He loved to talk about his teen years. We'd sit wide-eyed around the campfire as he talked about smoking weed, dropping acid, and how much booze he'd consumed on a particular night. He also loved to brag about his sexual exploits. These stories were exciting to young teenage boys anxiously waiting to become experienced men. I especially enjoyed how he described evenings with his lady friends. After all, I was fifteen! I suppose if our parents knew about that they'd have been none too pleased. One night, Judy felt sick and went to sleep early. Someone suggested convincing Craig to buy a few cases of beer. Eventually, after quite a bit of begging and pleading, he relented. I am embarrassed to admit it, but that night would be my first, but definitely not last, taste of beer. He also smoked a little weed with a few of the boys, but I was way too naïve at the time to partake. Looking back on it, I'm surprised there wasn't any backlash from all of this fun. Still, for me, the best of this trip was yet to come.

A few days later we were all basically recovered. We'd spent a morning riding particularly hard. Vermont, in case you didn't know, is basically one hill after the other. It always seemed like there were more ups than downs. Some days the constant climbing and descending was fun. Other days, especially hot ones, it could be very challenging. This particular day was hard on our legs; a killer headwind and too many hills made it an especially strenuous morning. We'd probably ridden for four or five hours, maybe fifty miles, when Judy suggested we stop for lunch. Little did I know this lunch break would be a major turning point and my life would change drastically. I never thought it would happen on this bike tour, but sometimes in life things just don't go as planned.

We dismounted our bikes outside a general store and walked around a bit to get the feeling back in our legs. It had been a hot morning so everyone was sweating, hungry, and thirsty. Soon enough Craig said he was going inside to buy us lunch. He mentioned something about an Italian Combo, which I'd never heard of before. I was famished so it sounded great! We all nodded and found our places at picnic tables or under the shady trees. I ended up sitting on the ground in a somewhat secluded corner with Judy discussing the morning ride. The others had occupied the picnic tables. Judy and I had found a relatively shady area on the ground beside the shop. The cool breeze was so refreshing. I noticed the long braid in her hair. It ran all the way down her back. She had taken off her shoes, socks and top shirt. For a boy my age it was exciting to steal a look at her breasts and firm bottom. She stared deeply into my eyes and both of us felt something, a hunger, a connection. It was obvious something was about to happen, and the anticipation was getting the best of us. Our small talk faded into an eerie silence. As we gazed at each other I wondered what it was going to be like. Were we really going to share this moment together, privately, away from the rest of the group? I could not remember ever being so close to an older woman like this. Craig interrupted us returning with a big box of sandwiches and cold drinks, then he left us alone. Maybe he sensed it? In front of us were two giant heroes and two drinks, lunch for two. Nobody noticed what was happening between us and it made it even more exciting. We sat close to each other, maybe our shoulders were touching. I watched nervously as Judy slowly moved her hand towards me. It would be just a matter of time before she made her move. "Are you ready to go for it?" she whispered. I could hardly stand it anymore. She and I leaned towards each other in unison. I felt her soft, sweet breath on my face. I noticed her pink lips close to mine. I watched, timidly, as she used her tongue to moisten them, awaiting what was coming. It was obvious, she was ready, too. Was this really happening to me, a fifteen-year-old? Her hand moved towards my upper thigh as her fingers wrapped around one of the massive heroes. She handed it to me. I responded by doing the same. She smiled. Slowly, carefully, we removed one another's sandwich wrapper. Our faces were inches apart. In a matter of seconds our mouths and lips would be satiated. We could no longer hold back. For a second, time stood still, then, simultaneously, both of us thrust forward, clutched the sandwiches, and . . . took a bite.

Wow, what a tasty sandwich! This was my first ever Italian Combo. Salami, pepperoni, provolone and a meat called capicola. The hero bread was overstuffed with these incredible Italian meats, lettuce, tomatoes, onions, jalapeños, and the best vinaigrette I ever had. There may even have been a few black olives as well. I couldn't believe something could taste this good. We tried to eat slowly at first, but our animal instincts took over and we devoured the sandwiches. She laughed and made fun of me when I told her it was my first time. I remember it well. Sure, we were hungry, but this sandwich was incredible. How could my mom have limited me to tuna and PBJs all these years when this combo was out there?

Lunch came to an end and the group slowly began moving toward the bikes. We had a ways to go before this day was over. Another twenty miles or so. By then, Judy had put her top shirt back on and would reenter her role as lead rider. We'd shared quite a moment together. We glanced at each other and smiled slightly. We didn't want the others to know what had just happened. It was our little secret. Not her first time, but mine for sure. We shared a look. Both of us hoped it might happen again before the tour was to end. We'd find a spot on the grass after a hard morning ride and eat a delicious Italian Combo.

What did you think I was talking about?

ITALIAN COMBO[2]

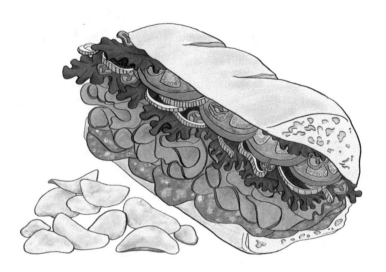

I worked at a Greek pizzeria that used to put all sandwiches in the oven for ten minutes. The Italian Combo may be even better hot! The sandwich is standard in most, if not all, sandwich shops.

INGREDIENTS

4–8, 10- or 12-inch heroes (depending on appetites!)

½ pound Genoa salami

½ pound pepperoni

½ pound spicy capicola

½ pound sharp provolone cheese

1 head lettuce, chopped

1 large tomato, sliced

1 small red onion, sliced

½ cup red roasted peppers, sliced into thin strips

½ cup chopped black olives (optional)

¼ cup red wine vinegar

1 T Dijon mustard

1 lemon

¾ cup extra virgin olive oil

Salt, black pepper, and dried oregano

INSTRUCTIONS

To make dressing, put vinegar in food processor with Dijon mustard. Squeeze juice from half a lemon into processor. Turn on and slowly add olive oil. The dressing should thicken slightly. When finished add a pinch of salt, pepper, and oregano to taste. Put dressing in squirt bottle.

Slice open the heroes and lay flat. On bottom half of bread place chopped lettuce. Squirt a liberal amount of dressing on each sandwich. Layer roasted peppers, black olives, tomatoes and red onions.

Now that the base of the sandwich is prepared, layer the provolone so the entire sandwich has cheese. Layer the salami, pepperoni and spicy capicola. This should be a big sandwich. If you want a real taste sensation, try adding mayo and spicy mustard. Place top half of bread on to complete sandwich. Cut each sandwich in half or thirds.

Plate and serve with Wise Onion and Garlic chips.

CHAPTER 7
THE SANDWICH MACHINE

For the past twenty-five years I've worked alongside a sandwich machine. The machine takes up very little space at the sandwich station. What it lacks in size it makes up for in production. Day after day, year after year, around lunchtime, the sandwich machine turns on and begins to crank out sandwiches. It doesn't work on electricity but on obsession, perfect sandwiches time after time, and no skimping on ingredients. The overstuffed sandwiches roll out of the machine at an incredibly fast pace. I'll monitor as roast beef, turkey, tuna and chicken salad sandwiches are churned out on assorted breads and rolls. Veggies, cheeses, and dressings are generously applied and that salty, all-time favorite topping, bacon, is always crisp. For some reason the machine favors mayonnaise but will also spread Russian dressing, cranberry sauce and any number of mustard types. With reckless abandon the machine processes orders and completes them almost always mistake-free from the beginning of lunch until every customer has been satisfied. Working next to the machine has been an honor and a privilege. Just recently the machine has finally begun to slow down, if only slightly. Years of daily work have taken a toll and several parts have been damaged, replaced, or even removed. I watch in awe, despite the damaged and missing parts, how the machine still hardly misses a day. It might begin a little later and finish a little sooner, but the day is not complete without the machine at my side churning out sandwiches, even for a short time. Lucky for me the sandwich machine is not quite ready to shut down for good. There are still a few more good years in those gears.

Where did the machine come from, does it have a name? Yes, the

sandwich machine is none other than my mom, Phyllis. I gave her the nickname of "sandwich machine" about five years ago, and she earned it. Way
back when, before we worked together, my mom made sandwiches for me.
The machine was simply warming up for what was to come. I've never met
anyone as committed to making sandwiches as my mom.

When I was young my childhood was fairly typical. Dad went to work
and Mom stayed home to raise three children, and later adopted a fourth.
As a Jewish mother of three she took pride in feeding us. Breakfast was usually cold and dinner was always hot. Lunch was a different story. Lunch
was for sandwiches, most often peanut butter and jelly. Mom's PBJ was my
favorite thing to eat as a child. In addition, Mom always packed us a lunch
for school. No way were her children going to eat cafeteria food. We headed
to school with a brown bag in hand just about every day, a bag of chips, a
piece of fruit, and always, always a PBJ. On weekends we could count on
lunch promptly at noon. We'd come to the table and, on a plate waiting
for us, was a sandwich, naturally. Sometimes we had roast beef or turkey
on the weekends. Growing up Jewish, I never tasted ham, but turkey or
roast beef, served on a roll with mayo, lettuce, tomatoes and a few chips on
the side, made the perfect Saturday afternoon lunch. I recall that on long
car rides to visit relatives, Mom would insist on packing a bag lunch with
sandwiches, drinks, and snacks. Usually my sandwich was finished before
we reached the highway! Later, hours into the ride, I'd stare at my sisters as
they slowly unwrapped their sandwiches. Why didn't I save half? On plane
rides we were usually the one family eating just after take-off. We were not
about to wait for the food cart, it was sandwiches all around. I, for one,
was hooked on sandwiches at a young age and still am today. There's a certain irony that my adult life would revolve around the sandwich. I can
thank my mom for that.

I never tired of Mom's sandwiches. In fact, I think I came to expect
them and was a little spoiled. I'd worked in restaurants and taken cooking
classes in my teen years, but still appreciated coming home to find a sandwich

waiting for me at lunchtime, or anytime. Obviously, I could make my own sandwiches but why deprive Mom of such pleasure? Besides, they always tasted great!

One of my early jobs was at a busy restaurant working as a busboy. The work was hard, and the job ended late at night, usually well after midnight. I'd return home between 2 and 3 a.m., famished and still a bit wired from the night's activity. With sleep hours away and the rest of the house quiet I'd open the fridge and look inside. Mom made it a point to leave me rolls, lettuce, tomatoes and all other necessary ingredients to make a late-night sandwich. Usually I'd find tuna, turkey, or chicken salad. I'd make my sandwich and inhale it while watching a little television, then shower and go to bed. Looking back on those nights I bet Mom was in bed smiling to herself knowing she'd managed to feed me, even while sleeping.

When we made the decision to invest in a sandwich shop, with a gleam in her eye and a contagious enthusiasm, Mom proclaimed her expertise in sandwich making. Raising three kids had been excellent training, she thought. She could easily make sandwiches to satisfy even the most discerning customers. When I was growing up and in school, working with my parents never crossed my mind, especially with my mom, but from our early days in business to today, she has been an inspiration. I recall one night during the holidays when our catering orders kept us busy at work until nearly midnight. Mom told me to go home while she finished up with one of our employees. I arrived back at work the following morning at 6, armed with just a few hours of sleep and a dozen doughnuts. I fully expected Mom to sleep late. Just a few minutes after I began work I looked up to see her coming through the door, smiling, appearing well-rested, and fully prepared to begin work. She never shies away from long hours or hard work and has always been completely devoted to our success. Sure we have a disagreement every so often, but the dissension never lasts too long. There's no time to be petty when a line of twenty or so hungry customers are waiting for lunch.

I call it sandwich therapy: by the time the line has dissipated we've forgotten all about the disagreement.

Mom's dedication to our success truly shined at Gourmet Galley in Greenwich. Everyone on Greenwich Avenue loved her. There was even one customer who described her as the "belle of the avenue." Sometimes her devotion bordered on lunacy. Dad had taken her on vacation to Colorado for a week's ski trip one winter. First day on the slopes mom sprained her ankle. Unable to ski, she hopped the first plane back to Greenwich. She told Dad to finish the week on his own, there were sandwiches to be made back east. I asked her why she came back and she said she could feel a busy week coming and wanted to help. On another occasion, after surgery, the doctor instructed her to stay off her feet for at least two weeks. We didn't think she'd last two hours! Anyway, within a day or two she hobbled in to work and took her position on the sandwich line. I gave her a look, but figured it was pointless to suggest she recuperate. That's total sandwich devotion.

Today, after all these years, Mom still arrives each day to help with lunch. She says her day is just not complete without spending time on the sandwich line for an hour or two. I actually think it's in her genetic make-up and I've been the lucky, or unlucky depending on who you ask, recipient of these sandwich-obsessed genes. We continue, every day, side-by-side, making sandwiches and satisfying hungry customers at lunch. One day, about five years ago, I began designing a new menu. With all items laid out in place I had one page to spare. I could not think of adding any more food items as the menu was already packed. It occurred to me that the menu lacked personality, a little something to tell customers who we are. I decided the best thing to do was give everyone nicknames and have a page of caricatures. The entire staff was represented. It came out great. My wife designed it, and it was colorful and funny. Our employees and customers loved it. I had "Grill Master," "Salad King," and a few more. Under the picture of my mom, in black letters, reads, "Sandwich Machine." The perfect nickname.

PEANUT BUTTER & JELLY[3]

Where it all begins for many of us. With so many jellies, jams, and assorted nut butters out there, it's still a combo that can't be beat!

INGREDIENTS

1 loaf of white (or wheat) bread

1 jar of peanut butter (or any nut butter—almond is great)

1 jar of jelly (raspberry is an excellent choice)

½ gallon milk (the only beverage suitable for PBJ)

4 tall glasses

INSTRUCTIONS

Lay four slices of bread flat on counter. Spread a layer of peanut butter on each slice followed by a layer of jelly.

Top each slice of bread with another slice and repeat previous instruction. Once you have a second layer of peanut butter and jelly, top off each sandwich with one more slice of bread. What's better than a PBJ? A double-decker PBJ!

Slice each sandwich into two equal triangles and pour 4 large glasses of milk.

Plate and serve along with milk and Lay's Classic potato chips.

CHAPTER 8
THE UNKNOWN EMPLOYEE

The hiring process has always been the bane of our existence. I can't speak for others in our industry, but everything from placing ads to interviews to the suspenseful first day of work has often been an exercise in futility. It never has been and never will be an easy task. Most, if not all, of our employees do not commit to a lifetime of kitchen work, creating job vacancies in our shop from time to time. Sure, some have been with us many years, but those cases are few and far between. In fact, one employee turned partner of mine, Santiago, actually married my younger sister, Allie. Now that's commitment. He's been a part of the business for eighteen years or so. Plus, he's still married to Allie, and they have three kids. There's another type of worker, the type that never lasts. The polar opposite of those who've been on our staff for years. What about them? They are the almost-employees who diligently answered an ad online or, years ago, in the newspaper and decided they wanted or needed a job. They made the phone call and even showed up for the interview. What happens next never ceases to amaze me. I refer to this group as "The Unknown Employee."

Our interview process tends to be about as easy as they come. We prefer to do it in person, but, in times of desperation, the phone call will suffice. The line of questioning begins with name and often ends with, "When can you start?" Most times there are no other questions. We even skip the last name and address. Those details can wait until the first day of work, if it ever comes. Sometimes I think our ads should be as simple as, "Warm body needed for kitchen, experience helpful." Very seldom do employees leave and give proper notice. Some employees have actually left in the middle of the workday. They simply go out for a smoke and never come back. Not even a courtesy cell phone call as they drive away. A driver we had once went out for a delivery and never returned. The only reason we knew he quit was because a tow truck pulled up in front of our store with the Gourmet Galley van attached, found in a ditch. At least the driver had the decency to call for the tow. At this point we need someone, and fast. The thing about the food service business that differs from other services is that procrastination is not an option. Today's lunch cannot be served later or tomorrow. There's a certain degree of urgency and the work can't wait. It's time to hire someone new.

On interview day, often times a prospective employee brings along a buddy. I've never understood why an adult thinks it's a good idea to bring a friend to a job interview. It just seems so dumb. As we sit down the "John Doe" alongside thinks he should be involved as well, like an agent or something? Usually we instruct the friend to wait outside. After a brief intro, the prospective employee informs us how he really needs a new job, then often begins to boast about years spent in food service and how little or no training will be necessary: a certain red flag. Some even come with a very, very long list of restaurants they have worked in before, which is a definite red flag. The longer the list, the less likely the person will work out. Their work ethic, they assure, is top notch and they rarely, if ever, miss work days. That is red flag number three. Some want to start right away, but most need a few days to get ready. Also a red flag. Another red flag, they all want to know their salary before the interview. Perhaps there are multiple job offers on the table for this guy. We ask for, but don't usually receive, references. Once, a prospective employee actually gave us a reference. Turns out his was a drug dealing thug. No references, bright red flag. As these red flags fall, like leaves in autumn, out of desperation we hire The Unknown Employee. Here's where it all comes apart.

A start date and time are set and a salary is agreed upon. We shake hands and get one last assurance that they will show up. Most of the time the start date is the next day, though we've had success hiring people on the spot—start date, now! Those, believe it or not, often work out. I guess they don't have time to think about it. At the point of hiring a sense of relief comes over us as we figure we have found someone to fill the void. Even if the new employee isn't great, at least they will take some of the pressure off just by being there. A warm body is better than no body, most of the time! The start day arrives with a renewed sense of hope. Maybe this new guy will work out? The clock moves. A few minutes before the specified time I begin to worry. The first day of work, shouldn't they show up ten minutes early? Then start time, still nothing. We stare at the door. Every time the door opens a feeling of relief and brief euphoria is followed by a sinking feeling, just a customer, again. Always the optimist, I give it an extra ten minutes, after that, reality sets in. Another no-show. The Unknown Employee strikes again.

Sometimes, when they do show up, in ten minutes we wish they hadn't. Regarding new employees, we can tell within the first few minutes, maybe seconds, whether or not they have what it takes. Certain mannerisms, hygiene habits, and personality traits put a stamp of approval, or disapproval, almost immediately on their future employment. If a new employee shows up a half hour late, they may as well not bother. If a new employee arrives with torn jeans and a dirty shirt, we'll probably ask them to leave, unless we are *reeeeeally* desperate. Did that once, major regret, it lasted a week—a week of paint-stained pants and shirts with holes was enough. If a new employee just moves slowly and doesn't react to simple instructions, probably won't work out either. These types of employees usually just leave, like ghosts disappearing into a dark night, like they never even started— the Unknowns. They claim to have forgotten something in the car and, mysteriously, never appear again. I recall a new employee nicking his finger with a knife the first hour of work. He then took a half hour applying a bandage before deciding he was weak from too much blood loss and could no longer work. If a new employee does make it through a busy lunch, they'll gladly make themselves a big sandwich, then choose to eat it in their car. Not even a thank-you for the sandwich. I assume they leave tire marks on the road when leaving.

Sometimes, rather than being a no-show and a no-call, The Unknown Employee has an excuse. Here are a few beauties from over the years along with my thoughts.

—"I can't find my car keys." The all-time classic excuse.

—"I don't have change for the parking meters" (50 cents a day at the time). If they'd asked, I'm sure I would have loaned them the 50 cents.

—"The bus didn't show up." That happens a lot. I guess the city of Greenwich only runs one bus a day, and if you missed it, too bad, another one will come tomorrow. Although, presumably they missed that one too.

—"I got another job." This one I might even believe sometimes. Once an Unknown walked out after a half day. A few days later I called him. We owed him a half day's pay. He said his new job kept him too busy to stop by, ever. Never saw him again. He got one of those 24/7 jobs I guess.

—"I had to take my dog to the vet, he fell down the stairs." Funny, any time one of my dogs fall down the stairs they get up and shake it off.

—"I'm getting a bad vibe from this place" (our shop). I have no answers for that one.

The litany of excuses can be amusing, but at the same time sad. These are adults, some with children.

The question "Why?" comes to mind during these situations. Why call and discuss the job? Why come to the interview and accept the job? And, why don't they show up? I've developed a few theories over the years. Maybe The Unknown Employee likes the idea of looking for work, but does not like the actual work. They feel going from interview to interview accepting jobs is work. Too bad they can't get paid for that. Maybe, after the interview, they were so thrilled about the job and pending salary that they went out and bought a lottery ticket, and they won. No need for a job. And, last, maybe they woke up fully prepared for the first day, headed out the door, and, on the way to work, got hit by a bus. Kind of a gruesome depiction, but you never know. I never thought to call the emergency room. After dozens of unknowns over the years, I don't have any good answers to the question why, why, why don't they show up? At least we never had to pay them, and we never really remember their names.

A MEXICAN TORTA

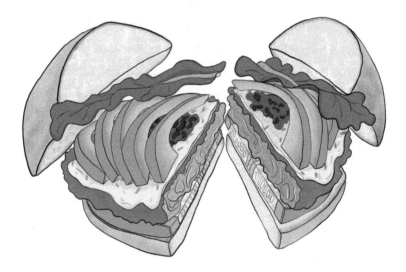

This delightful Mexican-style sandwich can be made with chicken or steak. I've always made it with spicy chicken cutlets. Try heating the entire sandwich in the oven.

INGREDIENTS

    4 8-inch heroes
    4 pieces thinly sliced chicken cutlets
    1 12 oz. can of black beans
    1 head chopped lettuce

1 sliced tomato

1 sliced avocado

½ cup jalapeño rings

1 pound cotija cheese (shredded cheddar is a good substitute)

1 cup seasoned bread crumbs

1 T cayenne pepper

½ cup real mayonnaise

2 eggs

2 T olive oil

INSTRUCTIONS

Whisk eggs together in a small mixing bowl and add chicken. Mix bread crumbs with cayenne pepper. Place bread crumb mixture on plate and, one at a time, dredge each cutlet, completely coating them.

Add olive oil to skillet and fry chicken cutlets until cooked through and internal temperature reads 165 degrees. When complete, slice open heroes and lay flat.

Spread mayo on bottom half of each hero and layer lettuce, tomatoes, jalapeño rings, avocado and chicken cutlets. Top off with cheese.

In food processor, blend black beans until they become a spreadable paste. You may have to add a little water.

Spread the bean paste on the top half of each hero and put bread in place on top of sandwich. Cut in halves.

Plate and serve with Lay's Hint of Lime Tostitos chips.

CHAPTER 9

YOU'RE FIRED! ER...NO WAIT! COME BACK!

Firing, or termination, has been a part of our business since the start. It's rarely an easy thing to do. Working in the food service business is hard. When an employee is hired they usually understand what the job entails. The hours are generally long and conditions in the kitchen can be brutal. Depending on the time of year, kitchens can be either uncomfortably hot or uncomfortably cold. Imagine working in a kitchen that's so cold in the winter you can actually see your breath while prepping breakfast. Summers are no better, as temps can rise well over 100 degrees in the middle of July. Standing over a five-foot-long flat-top grill in the middle of summer, cooking chicken, steaks, and burgers, is like standing on the sun. In addition, there's the salary and benefit situation. We try to keep our salaries in line with industry standards, well above minimum wage, but it's not a fortune. The benefit of working for us is simple: if you do your job well, you can come back tomorrow and do it again! Sometimes I wonder why anyone would want to work in food service. Despite all of this, we've had many employees over the years come and go. Some have been great and we've even kept in touch with them as they have moved on to other careers. Others, not so much, and some, unfortunately, have been fired.

Termination is almost always a last resort for small-business owners. We pay unemployment taxes like everyone else, so if legitimate claims are made by a recently terminated employee, the tax rate increases. By the way, I've only once in my career addressed a legitimate claim. Occasionally, during the ups and downs of the business cycle, it's necessary to make cutbacks. Knowing that this happens in many industries doesn't make the termination any easier. We've only had to do this a handful of times over the years, and choosing the employee to release from duty is painful, especially if the current crew is generally strong. After long internal debate we decide what to do. In this case, most of the time, the employee sees it coming and understands. There's always an assurance that when things pick up they are welcome back, though I can't recall anyone who actually waited around for this to happen. We are happy to give the employee a recommendation and they usually find work in a few days. The food service industry is known for high turnover, so jobs open up all the time.

Other times, termination is our only choice. Issues like absenteeism, tardiness, or poor behavior on the job will most likely lead to termination. Years ago we hired someone with anger management issues. One day, in a fit of anger, he damaged the back door of our shop. We had no recourse but to terminate. When the former employee attempted to make an unemployment claim, it was denied due to his behavior. Another time, years ago, we suspected an employee was stealing. We considered setting up a minor sting operation to catch her in the act. One night we cleverly devised a plan we thought would catch her red-handed, or turkey-handed as it were. Just before we were to implement the plan, another employee reported that food was disappearing into the pocketbook of our suspected thief. Rather than get involved in a complicated situation, we decided to shelve our plan and terminate the thief before things got worse.

Believe it or not, some employees attempt to bait us into firing them. Perhaps they like drama or plan to collect unemployment. It usually doesn't work and employment always ends suddenly. We had a kitchen worker who was with us for several years and was excellent, until his last week or so. One week, out of the blue, his attitude changed and his productivity dropped off. Instead of performing his job as he had for many years, he spent his time mostly talking and taking restroom breaks. Soon enough, on the next busy day, I asked if he wanted the job anymore. He kind of stared at me, daring me to give him the gate. With the phone ringing and customers waiting, I decided it was no use. As I pointed towards the back door and began to fire him, he was already gone, like the roadrunner, no need to look back. I never found out what happened to him.

One firing in our history, however, was amusing, amazing and unbelievable.

Tony, originally from Peru, started out as a dishwasher. As with many of our kitchen help, he was a cousin's friend's nephew's uncle. Finding employees has never been easy so we often rely on asking current employees if they have friends or family. This strategy can work out great but can also be disastrous. In this particular case, it was working out fine. Then it all changed. That's where this story begins.

One day, a Tuesday, Tony, for some reason, decided not to show up for work. There was no phone call, no warning, just a no-show. Being in the food service business means adapting to ever-changing situations, fast. Within a few hours we'd found a new dishwasher, a cousin of a current employee. It was extremely fortuitous because there were stacks of dishes to wash, some left over from the previous day. I didn't want to wash dishes all day and I could probably speak for everyone else in the kitchen. So the new guy arrived and things settled down. The mountain of dishes that had built up all morning had diminished and he'd gotten the hang of the dishwashing machine, which was constantly breaking down. In addition, he had a great attitude and worked quickly—two of the most important traits to have in food service. The day finished up and still no word from Tony. At that point, we figured his days at Gourmet Galley were finished.

At the time, nobody knew that he'd spent the night in jail for something he didn't do. It was a wrong place/wrong time and stupid friends situation that got him incarcerated overnight.

The next day, at around 8 a.m., I happened to look up from my work and, standing in front of me was, you guessed it, Tony. He was dressed for work, clean shaven and ready to start the day. I kind of pointed in the direction of the dishwashing area and there was our new employee elbow deep in soap suds completely engulfed in his work. Tony spoke very little English,

44

but I understood the look. It said, "How could you fire me?" But no explanation was necessary. Dejected, Tony hung his head and began to slowly walk out of the kitchen. I went back to work.

That was that. Tony was gone, another ex-employee.

Just then, one of the kitchen staff noticed the salad maker, Juan, was over an hour late. Did he quit? Did he decide to pursue another career? He didn't even call. At that point we couldn't care less. We needed a salad maker. I saw the back of Tony's head as he was nearly through the door. "Stop him," I yelled. Someone got his attention and he turned around. I waved him back. It was as if he'd been reborn. We needed him to work, right then. His arrival back in the kitchen was greeted with a huge sense of relief. Our search for a new salad maker was a short one. Not only were we thrilled he didn't leave, he got a promotion. Who would have thought? Only in the food service business can you not show up for work, get fired, get rehired and get a promotion all in the span of twenty-four hours. And Juan (remember him?) never resurfaced again.

As a salad man, Tony quickly learned the job. By the end of his first day he was making salads like a pro. Apparently, while washing dishes all those months, he was taking copious mental notes on the kitchen work. He observed how things were done and was ready for food prep when called upon. He was stationed next to a repulsive line cook who had a penchant for absenteeism. Soon enough, Tony was doing double duty as a salad man and a grill man. There were days when it seemed he was running the entire kitchen by himself. He simply learned what to do by watching and got better at it than everyone else. Over the years, it has amazed me that Tony never, ever loses his cool at the grill. We could put twenty orders in front of him and he calmly, coolly gets it all done. Remarkable really, it's a trait I've envied for years. I found it calming having Tony in the kitchen. He's probably my favorite import from Peru. Tony worked for us many, many years and became one of our best employees. He trained himself to be a grill master. To think we almost let him get away . . .

PERUVIAN CHICKEN SANGUCHON[5]

Great sandwich to make with rotisserie chicken. You can substitute leftover turkey.

INGREDIENTS

> 4 soft brioche rolls
>
> 1 rotisserie chicken
>
> 4 large lettuce leaves
>
> 1 tomato, sliced
>
> 1 avocado, sliced
>
> 4 small servings of prepackaged French fries
> (about 10 fries per serving)

4 eggs

1 small onion, diced

1 small green pepper, diced

2 T mayo

Salt and black pepper

INSTRUCTIONS

Preheat oven to 375 degrees. Carefully separate the two breast halves from rotisserie chicken and shred with a fork or use your fingers. Put dark meat aside for another use.

Bake fries until ready and lower oven to 250 degrees. Add shredded chicken. Keep fries and chicken warm.

Cook the 4 eggs sunny side up in a frying pan. Cover with a lid to keep warm.

Open the four brioche rolls and lay flat. Spread mayo on one side of each roll. Layer the lettuce leaves, tomatoes, and avocado on the rolls.

Remove chicken and fries from oven. Evenly distribute chicken on the rolls and place one egg atop each. Finish off the sandwiches by adding fries to the top and sprinkling the diced onions and peppers along with a pinch of salt and pepper. Put on top of roll. Do not cut.

Plate and serve with Cape Cod Waffle Cut chips.

CHAPTER 10
YOU NEVER FORGET YOUR FIRST... JOB

I remember it like it was last week. A Saturday afternoon in early September and I had resigned myself to a night of relative boredom. Maybe watch some television, eat some ice cream. Usual activities of a fourteen-year-old at home. The phone rang and Mom said it was for me. Who could be calling me? An old baseball coach of mine, Scott, was on the line. Apparently, in his spare time Scott managed a local restaurant, a small seafood place downtown. Scott sounded desperate, and I would come to know that sound all too well over the next ten years.

"Do you want to come to work tonight, maybe make a little money?" he asked.

"What do I have to do?"

"Easy, just wash a few dishes," he said. It turned out later his definition of "a few" and my definition of "a few" varied somewhat.

I'd never had a job before and it hadn't occurred to me to work in a restaurant. Working for Scott would set the standard for all future jobs I would hold over the next few years, and a career I would pursue after college.

"Sure," I said. "Sounds like fun. What time do you want me to begin?"

"About a half hour ago!" he gasped.

I hung up the phone and asked Mom if it was all right. She was probably thrilled with the idea of getting me out for the night. We jumped in the car and took the short drive downtown to the restaurant. Scott rushed me into the kitchen. I took a look around. A large six-top burner stove sat in one corner. It held one of the biggest pots I'd ever seen. A deep-fryer was saddled next to the stove. A huge walk-in fridge was in the other corner, along with a freezer, a two-door, reach-in fridge, and a few other typical items one might find in a commercial kitchen. Most of this equipment I'd never seen before, but would come to know well in the years to come. Giant ladles, spoons, and spatulas hung from dirty hooks on the wall. There was even a boom box, covered in black soot with aluminum foil for antennas sitting near the lone window in the kitchen. It blared rock music all night. I would find one of these in every kitchen I ever worked. I even had one in the early days of Gourmet Galley until, one day in a fit of rage, I smashed it on the floor. (I may have had some anger management issues in my early twenties.) No more boom boxes after that!

I was in awe looking around this small kitchen. There was an energy I noticed and soaked in immediately. The air smelled like seafood and fresh vegetables. I didn't even ask how much I would get paid. I was indeed an innocent fourteen-year-old, probably not even at the legal age to hold a job, but child labor laws hadn't made their way to my town. Finally, Scott brought me to a three-bay sink that had a sprayer thing and a pull-down dishwasher. On the floor were rubber mats on which I stood all night. Cleaning them, I learned later, was a real bitch. The tiny holes filled with whatever leftover food happened to fall on the floor. After very little instruction I got to work.

The next six hours were a blur. There was a head cook, with a bandana on his head and really long hair. He had tattoos all over his arms, something I'd never seen before. He didn't say too much to me, only a warning: "I throw a lot of steaming-hot pots and pans your way so be ready to duck!" He was not exaggerating. At least a half a dozen times that night I was nearly clocked in the head by a flying pan. When I officially began work, dinner was under way and the kitchen was pandemonium. Waitresses were coming and going and food was everywhere—steamed fish, grilled fish, fried fish, salads, desserts, coffee and more. It was dizzying, but it was a fun challenge to keep up with the dirty dishes that kept on coming. Scraping the fish from the skillets was difficult, but I loved every minute. At one point I stepped back and took inventory of myself. My apron was covered in a combination of soap, water, fish sauce and ketchup. Nobody told me where the clean aprons were, and I was too afraid to ask.

At about ten o'clock, Scott came into the kitchen and asked me how it was going. I had a big smile on my face. "Can I get something to eat?" I asked. He looked at me like I was crazy.

"You mean you haven't eaten anything yet?" he asked.

He asked me what I liked and I said French fries and a soda. That would be a wholesome dinner. Before I knew it a large plate of fries was in front of me along with a tall glass of Coke. Large servings of Coca-Cola would become my go-to drink to get me through long, difficult nights at many restaurants in which I worked. I gulped down the soda and ate everything but the plate. Then, I got back to work. By then some of the waitresses had gotten used to me and began chatting as they passed by. One would warn me not to trust the manager or to beware of a particular line cook, while another might offer me a cigarette. They thought I was cute. I suppose they got tired of talking to the cook with the long hair and tattoos. The waitresses all had big hair, smelled like too much perfume and cursed a lot. Wow, this was what a restaurant kitchen was like! This place is great, I thought. At one point, a distressed waitress came running into the kitchen with a half-eaten piece of fish remaining on a plate. "There's an asshole at table five who says this fish is undercooked. He ate just about the whole goddamn piece already!" she said as she slammed the plate on the counter. The cook, visibly annoyed, tossed the fish back onto the broiler for a few minutes. "Here, hope he fuckin' chokes on it!" he barked. And off the waitress went back into the dining room. The restaurant kitchen, I quickly learned, was quite a scene. I even got the nerve up to talk to one of the assistant cooks about midway through the night. I recall asking him if this was a typical Saturday night. "Fuck yeah," he said. Yes, the waitresses, the manager, and now the cooks were providing me with my first lesson in restaurant language 101: use lots of four-letter words. I even tried dropping a few F-bombs later that night, to the delight of the kitchen staff. They saw serious potential.

At one point I looked over to watch the cook prepare lobsters. I'd never eaten lobster before, much less prepared one. It seemed so cool to me how he'd drop the crustacean into the boiling water and, in a few minutes, presto, the lobster was removed, bright red and ready to eat. It went out on a plate with some melted butter, lemon, and parsley, the latter I found out, used for garnish, not to be eaten. I thought someday I would try that on my own. A few years later, in the first cooking class I ever took I got my chance. The teacher, Mrs. Williams, informed us we could cook whatever we wanted for the final exam. Recalling my first job, I leapt at the opportunity to cook lobster. We made grocery lists and Mrs. Williams looked at me quizzically when perusing my list. I begged her, and she managed to fit one lobster into the budget. It made more sense than suckling pig, another classmate's first choice. The final class arrived; time for our meals to be prepared. As I prepped and cooked, I thought back to my first job. Mrs. Williams had to help me a bit, but, when we finished, I had a perfectly cooked lobster. I extracted all the meat and created a tasty lobster salad, which I then put on a few soft buns, with a slice of lemon. Even the cook from the restaurant would have been impressed.

Things eventually slowed down and I started to see the end of the dishes. The stacks brought in were smaller and smaller and I could see the cooks beginning to relax a little. We were all sweating profusely from the night's work. As I finished, I noticed an awful odor. I could not make out what it was, but after I finally powered off the dishwasher, I took off the apron I had been using. It smelled putrid—a combination of who knows what from where ran up and down the apron and had soaked through to my shirt and pants. Even my sneakers were soaked, and stank as well! I figured when I got home I could shower and change before a well-earned sleep.

It had been a great night, but I forgot to ask Mom to pick me up, and it was past midnight, too late to call her. The dining room was dark and the last of the kitchen staff was heading out for the night. I asked one of the cooks about Scott. He kind of shrugged. "Scott's long gone. Was that cock-sucker supposed to pay you?" he asked. I didn't know what to say. Was I going to get paid for my hard work? I was surprised he didn't even stop to thank me or say goodnight. Kind of a dick, since after all, I got him out of washing dishes for at least one night. (I did get paid the following week. Thirty dollars, and it seemed like a fortune.) I was on my own. Home was about a mile away, and I might have to walk. Since it was September, the night was still warm so, as my dad used to say, I decided to go on a shank's mare. As I walked home, I reflected on the last six hours. The atmosphere in the kitchen was like nothing I'd experienced. There was something about the action I loved. Was it the crazy cook, the waitresses, the fries, the cursing? It didn't matter. What mattered was I had a new job that was fun. As I walked along that night, cars passed by. I was a fourteen-year-old walking alone at almost 1 a.m.—you would think someone would stop! In a few minutes a car pulled up next to me. I peered in and saw parents of a friend. "Need a lift the rest of the way?" the father asked.

"Sure," I said, adding proudly, "I just finished my first night working at the seafood restaurant."

At that point I'd gotten closer to the car and was reaching for the door handle. He looked me over: clothes disheveled, hair a mess, and then he caught a whiff. His look said it all. The fish/soap/fries smell had encom-passed my entire being and there was no way he was letting me sit in his back seat. "Why don't you just jog the rest of the way?" he meekly suggested. "You're pretty close already." I got a glimpse of his wife and she was holding her nose.

"No problem," I said. I walked home, showered and went to bed.

LOBSTER ROLLS

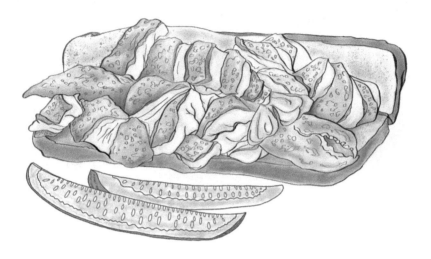

Especially good in summertime! I suggest buying the lobster meat, fresh if possible. Other than making sure the water is squeezed out, it's very easy to use.

INGREDIENTS

4 cups chopped lobster meat (leave it with lots of chunks)

4 top-split hot dog buns, lightly buttered and toasted

½ cup real mayo (maybe a little more)

2 coarsely chopped celery stalks

1 tsp black pepper

1 lemon cut into wedges

1 finely chopped bunch of fresh dill

(continued)

(continued)

INSTRUCTIONS

Put lobster meat in bowl and add mayo. Add chopped celery and black pepper and mix all together to form lobster salad.

Remove hot dog buns from toaster and fill each with a generous serving of lobster salad. Top off each roll with a sprinkle of fresh dill.

Along with lemon wedges, plate and serve with Cape Cod Kettle chips.

CHAPTER 11

HOW TO MAKE AND REALLY ENJOY A CUBAN SANDWICH

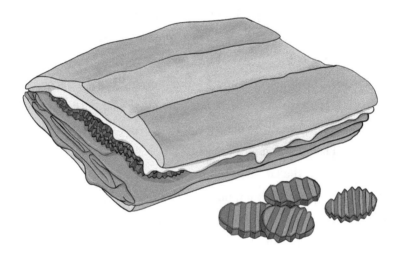

Making and eating a Cuban sandwich is like no other culinary experience. A Cuban is the combination of slow-cooked pulled pork, Swiss cheese, grilled ham, and a handful of other ingredients, which together create a masterpiece. After one bite, you crave more. The flavors bounce off your tongue and tingle your taste buds. I've heard people say they can't get to the next bite fast enough. How can a combination of so few ingredients taste so good? Quite frankly, it's almost orgasmic, and definitely addictive. Let me enlighten you. Step-by-step, I'll take you through the whole process. I'll describe the preparation, the smoking, the eating, and everything in between. As the cooking process winds down, the excitement and anticipation of your first bite will be almost unbearable. You will discover why the process of creating a Cuban sandwich is so delightful. So hold on tight, we're about to get started.

The ingredients are simple, but there are a few essentials before we get to them. I'll assume if you are ready and willing to make Cubans you have an outdoor smoker or grill with a smoker attached. I'll also assume you are cooking for at least a small group. The Cuban sandwich experience should be a shared one. You will need an aluminum tray, a spray bottle filled with apple juice, a meat thermometer and a whole lot of time. Proper slow-cooking of pork shoulder for a Cuban can take about ten hours. The few ingredients you will need besides the pork are boiled ham, Swiss cheese, pickle chips, mustard, fresh heroes, fried onions, and barbeque sauce. Your favorite brands will do. You will also a need few pairs of heavy-duty rubber gloves for when you pull the pork. Most important: bring a big appetite!

To begin, unwrap and rinse the bone-in pork shoulder. The shoulder will weigh roughly six pounds. At the same time, get your smoker going at about 220 degrees. Lightly season the pork with salt, pepper, and minced fresh garlic on all sides except the fat side. Rub the seasonings in the meat using both hands, slowly and methodically, until it is covered completely. Really feel the meat, run your fingers around it to truly appreciate the texture. You should be able to feel the bone inside. Lay the pork, fat side up, directly on the grill grates and close the lid of the smoker. I recommend starting this process early in the morning. Six a.m. is perfect. This will give it enough time to cook and cool down before you prepare it for dinner. It should remain smoking at 220 degrees for two hours. Now is a good time to take stock of your supplies. If you are missing anything, set aside some time to pick it up later.

While you wait out those first two hours, imagine just how good the sandwich is going to taste this evening. Pork slow-cooked to perfection. Tender, juicy and succulent. The smoking process is a sensual experience, long, slow and never rushed. One might say it's even erotic. Grilling steaks, chicken, or chops takes very little time, but pulled pork is a day-long activity, and should be savored. The aromas, the seasonings, the gauging of the temperature and tenderness all add up to a sensational cooking and eating experience.

Now that the first two hours are up, it's time to transfer the pork to the aluminum tray. Set it in the pan and spray it down with the apple juice. You should spray it hourly for the next six hours. The apple juice spray keeps the pork moist. Increase the temperature in the smoker to around 275 degrees and close the lid. You now have about eight hours, so you will wait and wait and wait some more. Since smoking pork is often done outside, I recommend doing it late spring into summer. There's plenty of light and it's perfect for a lazy day at home, especially during a vacation or long weekend.

Now that the pork is closer to being done, decide what you will serve with it. A few sides are all that's necessary, as you don't want to take the focus off the star attraction. Baked beans or corn on the cob are excellent. While you are figuring out the details of your meal, take a look at the pork every hour or so. Also, eat a light lunch. When it comes time to sink your teeth into that smoked-to-perfection pork, you want to have a serious appetite. An afternoon preparing pulled pork is a lot like one of Eugene O'Neill's plays. A long day's journey into the best sandwich ever. It seems like it will never end. Eventually, you will slowly insert the thermometer and it will read 190 degrees, the perfect temperature. Turn down your smoker and let the pork cool for about forty-five minutes.

Remove the pork from the grill and lay it on a cutting board. Save the juice in a container. Put on your rubber gloves and begin to tear the meat away from the bone. It should tear easily. Begin to shred it and place it in a bowl. When complete, pour some juice in the bowl and mix. If you have a dog, give him some of the pork scraps after everything cools down. However tempted, avoid giving him the bone. He may as well enjoy the pork with you, right?

The pulled pork is ready. Now you may make the sandwiches.

Fry a large onion in a pan, then add the pulled pork and barbecue sauce. In a smaller pan, fry the boiled ham slightly, a few slices for each sandwich. Slice open the heroes and spread your mustard evenly on both sides. Lay the pickle chips on the bread, followed by the pork, Swiss, then, last, the grilled ham. The heat from the pork and ham will melt the Swiss cheese. Cut the sandwiches in half to eat.

This is it. Before you eat, take a good look at the sandwich. Maybe take a picture. I've posted many sandwich pictures, and the Cuban always looks the best. This is more than just a sandwich; it is an experience. Take your first bite and let the flavors fill your mouth with delight. This sandwich should taste like nothing you've eaten before. Spicy, sweet, moist, so many different tastes resulting in the ultimate satisfaction. Soon the sandwiches will be finished, and reality will set in. Tomorrow's another day. Sit together and enjoy what's left of the day. That's the Cuban sandwich experience.

WILD CARD RECIPE
(how could I possibly write a sandwich recipe book without tuna?)

TUNA SALAD

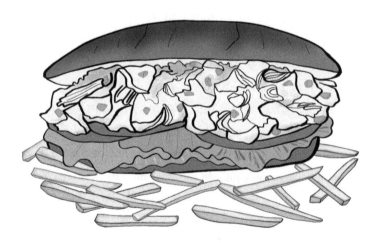

At Gourmet Galley we've been famous for our tuna salad dating back to the '80s, even before my family owned it. An old Greek man slowly and methodically made the tuna salad, which went directly into a large ceramic bowl in the deli case. It was our signature at the time. One day, a careless employee dropped the bowl and cracked it—a very sad day. A special service was held for it out in back by the dumpster. I could not have a sandwich recipe book and neglect tuna salad. Here is my favorite Sunday sandwich:

INGREDIENTS 7

4 8-inch heroes

3 6-ounce cans of solid white tuna, squeezed and drained

1–2 cups real mayonnaise

2 diced celery stalks

1 cup shredded carrots

Black pepper

¼ cup bread crumbs (will absorb extra water in tuna)

¼ cup honey mustard . . . yes, that's our secret ingredient!

4 large romaine lettuce leaves

1 large sliced tomato

1 jar extra-long pickle slices

1 small sliced red onion

INSTRUCTIONS

In mixing bowl combine tuna, celery, carrot, bread crumbs, and a pinch of black pepper.

If you make your own honey mustard, it's best to use spicy brown, not Dijon style. Mix 1 cup of mustard with ⅓ cup honey. It should be hot, sweet and easy to pour but not watery.

Add honey mustard and mix all ingredients. When well mixed add mayonnaise. Before making sandwiches, taste your tuna salad. The hint of sweetness makes all the difference.

Slice heroes but don't separate. Layer lettuce leaves, tomatoes, red onions, and pickle slices in center of bread, then add generous amounts of tuna salad. Close heroes and cut sandwiches in half.

Plate and serve with a large can of Pringles Original Potato Crisps. A tuna salad sandwich epitomizes lunch!

CHAPTER 12
THE BEST SANDWICH I EVER HAD

There are times we've all thought we just ate the best sandwich of our lives. Then, there are times we *know* we just ate the best sandwich of our lives. The following is for me one of those times.

In 2007, Mei and I got "Mauied" in the great state of Hawaii. Just the two of us on the beach with the minister, who was a former Ms. Hawaii, performing the ceremony. We found her services on the Internet. Hers was the only marriage service we found online that seemed a bit offbeat and fun. Others we came across seemed too traditional, designed for large groups and grand affairs. My fiancée and I agreed that a traditional type of wedding was out of the question.

Our wedding was scheduled for 10 a.m., July sixth, and we arrived on Maui very late on the fifth. With very little sleep, we got married on love and adrenaline, and after a celebratory lunch, slept most of the afternoon. The following morning my new wife and I attended a welcome breakfast at our hotel where a friendly hostess provided us with touring and sightseeing information, as well as a list of the best places to eat. Most of the information was useful since we were total strangers to the island. One bit of info stood out: a simple Hawaiian word, "ono." It translates as "tastes great," but is also the name of a fish native to Hawaii. She gave us the name of a sandwich shack that had a great ono burger. Her exact words were, "The ono is ono!"

Lunch was just around the corner, so we hopped into our rental car and headed in the direction of the sandwich shack. The volcanoes, the beach, snorkeling, even sex, could all wait. We had to try this burger, and fast. We pulled into the joint at around 11:30 and saw there was already a line. Let me tell you, when on vacation in Hawaii, there is no need to worry about time. This other-worldly island is a gift to be treasured and enjoyed, never rushed. We waited in line and, come our turn, ordered two ono burgers. After one bite it was apparent this was not an ordinary sandwich. Bite after bite, all we could do was smile at each other as we devoured the burgers. If this was Hawaii, maybe I'd never leave. The sandwich tasted so good: tender fish, red cabbage slaw, leaf lettuce and dill mayonnaise on a toasted burger bun. We agreed we should eat there at least a few more times before heading back to Connecticut.

A day later we planned a trip on the Road to Hana, a town in Maui known for sightseeing and natural pools. We were to wind back and forth about a hundred times en route to a true paradise. After a few stops for pictures we arrived and found the magical natural springs. We swam around a bit, relaxed, took more pictures and decided to head back to where we were staying. We had tickets to a show that night and did not want to be late. As luck would have it, we passed by the ono burger sandwich shack on the way back. My wife and I smiled at each other and made a quick decision: early dinner! "Let's grab a few more of those burgers," my wife suggested. We couldn't believe it. Do these sandwiches taste even better than before? We downed them in the rental car, and as we finished off the last few bites, we arrived just in time for the show to start.

For some reason we decided to explore other eateries for lunch the next few days. There was a fantastic burrito place, a sushi place, and we even tried the spam and eggs sandwich at Burger King. The spam was just as salty as it is everywhere else! We stayed in Hawaii for eight days and I can't remember one bad meal. Maybe it was from the high of being newlyweds or maybe food just tastes better on vacation. Whatever the reason, the two of us shared meals we've reminisced about ever since that trip, none more than the ono burger.

The final day of our trip was a bit depressing. Who wanted to leave this paradise? We'd gotten married and had seven days of pure ecstasy. We'd seen sights like never before and enjoyed a real luau on our last night. There was also quite a bit of newlywed activity, if you know what I mean. It was marital bliss, but it was time to get back east. Back to work, traffic, humidity, and the everyday grind to which we were accustomed. As we packed, we talked about how great everything was and how returning to the mainland was going to suck. Upon arrival at JFK, around 7:30 a.m., I would be heading straight to work. I grabbed our suitcases, full of goodies for everyone, from coffee to macadamia nuts, and placed them in the back of our rental car. My wife and I took one last look at the condo, our home for the past week, and got into the car. I pointed it towards the airport. Soon we reached a fork in the road, one way to the airport, the other to the ono burger stand. My wife turned to me and said, "Let's get one more."

Already worried about the flight I said, "I don't know if we have time. I don't want to miss the plane."

"Let's do it!"

I headed the car in the direction of the sandwich shack. We arrived and quickly ordered two ono burgers. "To go," I said, "all the way to Connecticut." As I sped to the airport Mei sat in the passenger seat and enjoyed her burger. She even managed to give me a bite or two. We arrived and the plane was boarding already. You've never seen two people run so fast through an airport to catch a plane. We made sure, however, that nothing happened to the final ono burger—precious cargo. I was hungry after all. By the time we got to the gate we were both panting and out of breath. Luckily, we were able to board and found our seats. We sat silently for a few minutes, then I reached over and whispered into my wife's ear something I would say quite a bit over the next few years. "I'm glad we stopped, you were right." As the plane took off and rose to flying altitude I slowly unwrapped my still-warm sandwich and took a few bites. Mei watched me eat at first. She gave me a look that begged for a bite. I relented, of course. She helped me finish it off. The best sandwich we ever had.

ONO BURGER

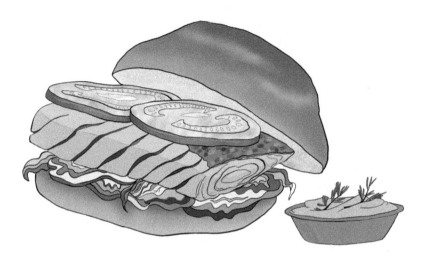

Ono is also called wahoo fillet. It is native to Hawaii and means "good to eat." If you have the good fortune to come across this fish and make this sandwich, you'll surely shout wahoo! It's best prepared on a grill but can also be cooked in the oven. Alaskan halibut may be an adequate substitute and might save you from having to fly to Hawaii!

INGREDIENTS

4 seeded hamburger rolls

4 1½-inch ono fillets

4 lettuce leaves

1 small head shredded red cabbage

¾ cup real mayonnaise

¼ cup sour cream

(continued)

(continued)

¼ cup heavy cream

1 T sugar

1 T red vinegar

Salt and pepper

1 finely chopped small bunch of dill

1 lemon

1 T olive oil

INSTRUCTIONS

Turn on gas grill to medium heat or preheat oven to 375 degrees. Sprinkle fish with salt and pepper and brush both sides with olive oil.

To make slaw, place shredded red cabbage in mixing bowl. Put ½ cup of mayonnaise in food processor and add the sour cream, heavy cream, red vinegar and sugar. The mixture should be smooth and creamy. If the mixture is too sweet, add a pinch of salt. Pour mixture over cabbage and mix well.

Mix the remainder of the mayo with the chopped dill.

Grill or bake ono fillets. The fillets are cooked when the inside is snow white and tender. Toast burger rolls on grill.

Place rolls on flat surface and spread dill mayo on bottom half. Layer the lettuce leaves and red cabbage slaw followed by the grilled fish. Squeeze a bit of lemon juice on the fish before placing top half of roll on sandwich.

Plate and serve with Cape Cod Dark Russet chips.

CHAPTER 13
BASTILLE DAY

Bastille Day is celebrated on July fourteenth, and is French National Day. It celebrates the storming of the Bastille, a fortress in Paris, in 1789 by the angry people of the city. There are many details, names, etc., surrounding this event that you may look up if it piques your interest. For the purposes of this story, just remember, *angry people storming*. "Storming" could be considered anything from throwing items, to breaking down barriers, to screaming, yelling and cursing. I was witness to all of this and more one Bastille Day in the mid-1990s.

It was a business-as-usual Friday in Greenwich, and we were preparing the food and beverages for the party we'd been hired to cater. A French company, one who had used us before, and was just down the road from our shop, wanted to celebrate Bastille Day. We had created a menu of Chicken Cordon Bleu and new potatoes with baguettes and Caesar salad. Petit fours and a large cake would be served for dessert. Champagne, Perrier, beer and water were all on tap. Dad was an excellent party set-up guy, so he and I arrived early to the location, and began getting everything ready. It was a sunny July morning and there was a company setting up a tent. The serving tables would go under the tent and the partygoers would sit at tables on the terrace outside the office building's main doors. From above the employees must have been observing us and getting excited about the party. It was Friday after all. What better way to finish a work week than with a company-sponsored party? The building rose up about five stories with a parking lot underneath, the only place that day to find shade. All was going as planned. The sweat poured off us as we set up tables, chairs, and linens. I didn't give it a second thought. I figured we were working hard. If I had taken a step back I would have noticed the terrace provided no protection from the sun and it was getting hot. In a few hours the partygoers would be eating and drinking under the hot, burning sun. In a few hours the terrace would also resemble the streets of Paris that fateful day in July 1789.

The morning progressed as the other staffers arrived. There would be about five of us, servers and bartenders. I noticed it was almost 1:30 and the party was to start at 2. As the food and drinks arrived, I ducked into the restroom to change. The sun had risen higher and the day was proving to be hotter than expected. My T-shirt was drenched in sweat, but I still was fairly carefree about the party. Things were moving along. As I headed back to the terrace to begin I saw one of the staffers, Emad, and we exchanged pleasantries.

"It's really hot under that tent," he said. "Must be about 110 degrees."

"We'll be fine, just drink a lot of water," I said.

As soon as Dad finished and began walking to his car the party started. More specifically, the people exited the building in a deluge onto the awaiting terrace and under the tent. Everyone was ready to party! It was nearly impossible to keep up with the demand of the anxious partygoers. We had three bartenders, including me, and could have used six. Champagne corks flew everywhere as we started pouring drinks for everyone. I actually nailed a guy with a major splash of champagne. He threatened to send me the dry-cleaning bill! His glare said it all; we were in for a difficult afternoon. Guests numbering 200 or so were ordering drinks two and three at a time. Plenty of beer, bottles of Perrier and glasses upon glasses of champagne were being ordered and consumed immediately. The partygoers were demanding but still reasonable at this point. The tent was hot and everyone, including the staff, was trying to stay cool by drinking. We held our own for a while. The food was being served and the party began to settle into a groove. At one point I took stock of the scene and things were hectic, but under control. Emad turned to me and said, "These people are really drinking a lot. It's so hot under the tent, imagine how it is under the direct sunlight." It was probably the hottest day of the year. There was plenty of water and ice, I thought, so nothing to worry about, right? Bastille Day was about to get under way.

"Holy shit!" one of the staffers yelled. I turned to look around and one of the staffers was in complete shock. "There's no more fuckin' water," he said. "Or beer, or champagne!"

"What about the cooler, and the ice?" I asked.

All gone, melted away. What could we do? There was not a single drop of beer, Perrier, Champagne, or water left anywhere and zero ice cubes. We had just run out of ice, water, and all other beverages on the hottest day of the year. The party wasn't even half over, and the sun refused to set. The sun's intensity baked the entire terrace. Things were about to get ugly. The heat was so intense and the day so hot that everyone just kept on drinking. One person, then two, then a third all began asking for water, not asking, demanding! We kind of stood there motionless as we tried to figure out what to do or say. I ran into the building to make a phone call. It felt nice to be in the air conditioning. I did consider hiding under a desk at that point. Maybe if I stayed inside long enough everyone would go home? I found a phone and called Dad at the store.

"Get some water, ice and soda here, an hour ago!" I exclaimed.

"It's busy here, can you wait?" he asked. I wish he could have heard the crowd at that moment.

"No way, get it down here, as much as possible!" I was yelling at this point. "We're about to lose total control!"

I exited the building and headed back to the tent. The tension was palpable and total pandemonium would soon ensue. In the tent were the staffers, like French guards cautiously waiting and hoping for some relief. On the terrace, just as in Paris, were the attendees, threatening angrily to overthrow the entire afternoon. This was truly becoming our own Bastille Day. Guests were yelling, screaming, and cursing for water, beer, or anything liquid. Long gone were the carefree partygoers who had arrived a few hours ago. They didn't even want dessert. The party was completely dry, and the natives were completely pissed off. In a few minutes I even watched as people heaved their empty bottles towards the trash receptacles. Though most ended on the ground, at least they didn't hit us. It was impossible to pacify this crowd. I tried, in vain, to explain that drinks were on the way. Nobody wanted to hear it. They were demanding beverages, *a present*. The tent looked like a war zone. At one point I thought the crowd was going to begin flipping tables in a form of protest. The food trays were empty and dozens of empty bottles of Champagne were piled, upside down, in the cooler once filled with ice. Dirty dishes were being dumped at the end of one table. Used silverware was strewn everywhere. Napkins and tablecloths had found their way onto the ground and littered the entire area. None of the staffers, like the French guards, knew what to do. One suggested we hide all the knives, just in case. She also grabbed the corkscrews and waved her hands in the air. "You never know," she said. The garbage cans were stuffed with dozens of empty Perrier and beer bottles. I heard plenty of profanity that afternoon in English and French! At long last, when almost all hope was gone, Dad arrived with several cases of water and soda. They were torn into and disappeared in seconds. I looked at him and shrugged. "Not enough water?" he asked. I slowly shook my head. "Not even close, this party was a real disaster," I answered sadly. "I thought they were going to kick the shit out of us!" I got back to work. The staffers were all working as fast as possible to clean up. We all wanted to put this nightmare behind us.

The sun began to set, literally and figuratively, on the party. Attendees started heading out; some went home while others planned to continue the party at a local bar. They stared us down as they exited. I got the feeling, in unison, they were wondering how in the world we didn't have enough drinks. Maybe the bars had enough water, beer, and soda. In silence we cleaned up the carnage. What began as a pleasant Bastille Day party about five hours before had disintegrated into a disaster we would not soon forget, and still talk about to this day on very hot days around July fourteenth.

Mom had stopped by towards the end to offer support. The party seemed to be a complete catastrophe. I wondered aloud if we'd even be paid. I saw her talking to the special events director of the company, the woman who originally planned the party. She was a petite woman with a fancy French name who spoke with a slight accent. Perhaps I was slightly dehydrated and a bit delusional, but it sounded like her last words to Mom as she headed to her car were, "Thanks, nice party, good food, next time bring more fuckin' water!"

JAMBON BEURRE[9]

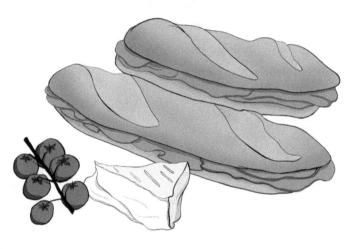

I included this French masterpiece because it relates to the Bastille Day story so well. It's delicious in its simplicity. As you enjoy it, imagine walking up and down the streets of Paris.

INGREDIENTS

> 2 ficelle French baguettes cut in 12-inch lengths (a small, very thin loaf of French bread)
> European butter, salted or unsalted, your preference
> 1 pound high-quality ham, sliced very thin

INSTRUCTIONS

Slice open baguettes and spread butter on one side or both sides (it's that good!).

Layer thinly sliced ham on each and close sandwiches.

Plate and serve with French's Potato Sticks.

CHAPTER 14
OH BABY

In the spring of 2013 my wife, Mei, and I had a baby girl. We named her Lillian, after my maternal grandmother. Mei came up with a Chinese character for her middle name and I still don't know what it means, or how to write it. She arrived weighing around nine pounds. I wasn't prepared for a baby back then and, some may say, I'm still not prepared. Despite my lack of experience as a parent, I've come a long way. Mei, on the other hand, is a natural. Being part of a big family with sisters, brothers, nieces, and nephews, she has had plenty of opportunity to hone her parenting skills. And being a teacher, I'm sure, has helped as well. The sandwich business, unfortunately, does nothing in the way of parental training with the exception of being able to make a good PBJ sandwich. It's hard to believe that, in my professional life, there has not been a single thing I've learned to assist me in becoming a good father. All that being said, when we discovered my wife was pregnant in the summer of 2012, I figured I'd better at least prepare myself to witness the birth. Nine months later, when Mei went into labor, all bets were off. I had no idea what to do.

On the morning of April 20, 2013, I was doing my usual prep at work. My wife was very pregnant so I thought it best to give her some alone time. It was a Saturday and I planned on working until noon. The shop would be closed that day. I would make a pot of chili, some basil pesto to be frozen, and prep roast beef for the following Monday. The day before, Friday, my wife had an appointment with the doctor. He said the baby would come any day and to be ready. I had to give Lillian credit for choosing a great day to officially enter the world. Nothing like a convenient child birth for the self-employed. When Mei called me with news of her labor at around 11, I even began to figure out if I was going to miss any work and asked what she thought. My wife still hasn't forgiven me for that. With more important things happening, I finished up and grabbed a few things that might be helpful. With snacks, drinks and sandwiches, my priorities were exactly where they were supposed to be. One of the sandwiches included was made with our oven-roasted turkey and corn bread stuffing. I've always loved that combination, especially with cranberry sauce and mayo. It reminds me of the day after Thanksgiving. I did not realize at the time that my wife would not be able to eat once she got to the hospital. At least one of us would not be hungry.

Mei's doctor told her that, after the onset of labor, it would be at least fifteen hours before she had to be at the hospital, so no need to rush. We had planned to have the baby in New York City, so we got ready and hopped in the car. My wife insisted on doing some last-minute shopping in Brooklyn and having one last meal of Chinese food for lunch in the afternoon. The sandwiches would be for later. As the day progressed, urgency began to set in. By nightfall we arrived at the hospital.

I highly recommend *not* having a baby in New York City. We spent a solid hour looking for parking. Fortunately, by the time we found a place to park, it was late and, since it was Saturday night, there were no meters. The doctor had instructed my wife to keep moving, so she walked around the halls of the maternity ward for about an hour. Always the supportive husband, I realized it was going to be a long night so I decided I'd better catch a few zzzs in the waiting room. Waiting room chairs are *not* conducive to sleep.

Finally, around midnight, we were in the delivery room. Once my wife was officially in labor, all eating ceased—for her at least. It had been a long day and I was starving. It seemed insensitive to eat in front of her, as she suffered through the first stages of labor, so I came up with a solution. Every few minutes Mei asked me for ice cubes. There were ice cubes in the bathroom, so I would duck in, grab a few cubes, and take a bite or two of my turkey sandwich, which I clandestinely stashed behind the door. It's an all-time classic and for good reason. When the stuffing is warm it's exceptional. Unfortunately, the hospital did not have microwaves in the room, but I managed with cold stuffing. Maybe I should have requested one! A bit of gravy for dipping would have been perfect, too . . . There was a moment when I debated asking my wife if I could head down to a 24-hour local deli for gravy, but I thought better of it, and decided to concentrate on the task at hand. By the way, I even munched on some pretzels. Little did I know the fuel I was taking in would prove invaluable as my workload increased by the hour.

Our doctor, Dr. Wei, was only half present at the birth. And that's a generous assessment. He was attending another birth just down the hall that was a more difficult delivery, in his eyes, so most of his time was spent away from us. The nurse assigned to our delivery was pleasant enough, but not very strong. A turkey sandwich might have helped her. When my wife needed assistance, yours truly was called upon to perform. I was in the end zone, if you know what I mean. I was not just an innocent bystander praying and waiting anxiously. Not only did I study the monitors to reassure Mei during the ups and downs of contractions, I actually watched up close on one of the monitors as the baby got herself in the position to be born. I worked hard that night. My wife, on the other hand, really worked hard. She insisted on natural childbirth resulting in pain like never before, so much that I am forever impressed with her toughness, strength, and perseverance. At one point she hinted to the doctor that she might consider an injection. He quickly dismissed her. "Too late!" he said, almost with a degree of satisfaction. I bet he felt like saying, "You wanted natural birth, you got it." In the meantime, I was able to eat almost an entire turkey sandwich and bag of pretzels.

As the night turned to morning, it seemed like the baby would never come out, perpetually stuck in the birthing canal. But finally, she was close to appearing, and we called down the hall to the doctor who had been with the other patient. He rushed in, and before he called the nurses, I said something like, "Hey Doc, I think the two of us can handle this on our own." He kind of looked at me like I was crazy and shook his head. Message received. Then, without underestimating the severity of what was about to happen, he took two steps, opened the door to the hallway, and yelled, "Shoulder!"

The clock read just past 11 a.m. when a team of nurses came rushing to the room. One nurse pushed me out of the way. Another nurse stood on the other side of my wife and still another got right behind the doctor. For a second or two I froze. It felt like an eternity as I watched the doctor, and his team of nurses, slowly ease our daughter out into the world. It was very impressive. My wife cried with joy and I came to the realization that, at that moment, I was a father. The doctor had me cut the umbilical cord to put my stamp on the delivery. In a few minutes someone handed me our daughter, Lillian. Beautiful baby, excellent sandwich! I was so thankful that I'd eaten that turkey sandwich because, at that moment, I realized that everything in life, including eating a sandwich, had just taken a back seat to our newborn daughter. The nurses took her away to perform the necessary post-birth exam and the three of us, Dr. Wei, my wife, and I, exhausted, enjoyed the snacks that remained in our bag.

MALTESE TURKEY[10]

One of the all-time Gourmet Galley classics. Eating this sandwich makes it feel like the day after Thanksgiving.

INGREDIENTS

8 slices marble rye bread

1½ pounds of sliced fresh roast turkey (dark or white meat, according to preference)

½ cup cranberry sauce (canned is fine)

½ cup real mayonnaise

½ pound unsalted butter

2 chopped celery stalks

½ chopped small white onion

6 sliced medium white mushrooms   *(continued)*

(continued)

1 corn muffin

5 slices day-old bread, white, wheat, or both, cut into small pieces

1 cup chicken broth

INSTRUCTIONS

To make stuffing, first melt butter in sauce pan. After melted, add onion, celery, and mushrooms. Sauté until veggies are cooked and limp. Add chicken broth and bring to a boil.

Crumble corn muffin in mixing bowl and add bread. Slowly add butter mixture and mix with spoon, or your hands. Careful, it's hot! Add enough so bread absorbs the butter mixture. The stuffing should be dry.

With stuffing still warm, lay rye bread on flat surface. Spread cranberry sauce on four slices and mayo on the other four. Place equal amounts of fresh turkey on four pieces of rye bread with cranberry sauce. Spoon out a serving of stuffing in the middle of each sandwich. Place the 4 slices of bread with mayo on top of each turkey and stuffing sandwich. Cut each in half.

Plate and serve. If you have warm gravy, use it to dip the sandwich! Add Rold Gold pretzels, too.

CHAPTER 15
THE CONVERSATION

Since my family started in the sandwich/catering business back in the early '90s, we've worked with dozens upon dozens of vendors. Vendors sell wholesale items, which we turn into retail items. We've had vendors for meat, produce, paper supplies, breads, bagels, bakery items, and even muffin batters. (Yes, at one point we baked our own muffins. That was a nightmare. I would bake a few dozen early in the morning. Some would burn, some would be sold, and others would be given to the staff at the end of the day, a complete waste of time. I did learn what a morning glory muffin was; tasty, but still not worth it.)

About fifteen years ago the need for vendors diminished considerably as the business was simplified. After our second move, we no longer had a restaurant with seating, and good riddance! If there ever was a portion of the business that we did poorly, it was the restaurant. Waitresses behaved like divas and customers were constantly complaining. It was impossible to explain that catering orders took preference. Then, with the rise of big box stores and restaurant supply houses, the need for vendors decreased even more. For small businesses such as ours, it became easier to self-serve when it came to most supplies. Pick-up was cheaper and more convenient. Anything we needed was a short drive down the road. Why have a middle man? That is pretty much where we, and most businesses like us, are today. We put aside a certain amount of time to shop every week. We make lists and are able to get just about everything we need locally. There are, however, a handful of vendors we simply can't, or don't want to do without. For example, we have a chip vendor, Mark, who has been servicing us for over twenty years. Mark comes to the shop once a week and spends about thirty minutes. Ten minutes are spent filling his chip rack and twenty are spent talking to us about sports, news, families, etc. He's always amusing. There's also a bread vendor, Frank, who, for nearly twenty years, has told us fascinating stories that he insists are completely true. I've heard most of them dozens of times and many of them involve booze, guns, or both. Most, if not all, are punctuated by poor English and plenty of four-letter words for emphasis. Frank's hair has been white since his forties, probably a result of his 1 a.m. wake-ups and seven-day work weeks. Someone once asked if he fought in World War Two (he is a former marine). Not even close, though his dad fought in Korea. He just looks a lot older than he is.

One vendor, though, has been with us since day one. He sells us name-brand sandwich meats and cheeses out of those big red and black trucks seen driving up and down major highways and in neighborhoods. He delivers the products that make our sandwiches possible. His name is Gerry and I would be remiss if I didn't include him as an important part of our sandwich history.

We met Gerry way back during our initial experiment in the food service industry: the meat, catering, and sandwich shop we operated for a little under two years in upstate Connecticut. Everyone, including vendors, employees, and customers, tried to take advantage of us and our inexperience, and most succeeded. Employees stole time and took advantage of our lenient style of management. There were so many vendors at that store it was hard to keep track. Bread vendors might sell products close to the expiration date, or produce vendors might overcharge for products because they knew we didn't have time to check. Gerry was the exception. Honest and hardworking with a real pride in customer service, Gerry was the only one we could completely trust. He actually took notice that we were working hard and, despite our early difficulties, maintained faith in us. He even offered advice, for free, on how to improve operations with menu suggestions and other ways to cut costs. After selling the business and buying

Gourmet Galley, it was the right thing to continue with his service and carry his products. It helped that what he sold was top quality, but in a business with little or no loyalty, having a vendor like him in our corner was a good idea. I don't think any of us ever dreamed the business relationship would last all these years.

Gerry was always a hustler. He said that even at an early age he created business opportunities and forged long-lasting relationships. As he got older he realized, like many of us, that working for someone else would not be his path to success. Some of us were just not built to work for others. After a brief search he came upon the business that has occupied his life now for more than thirty years. Like us, he is a lifer in the food service business and is completely dedicated to serving his customers. I recall countless times when he'd show up at our shop on a Saturday night, or even Sunday morning, to deliver product we needed immediately. Since our businesses are similar, it's been easy to bounce ideas off each other. We share some issues, so it's not uncommon to vent frustrations to each other from time to time. Losing a customer, chasing money, and employee problems, all reflect the commonality of our work lives, especially the money part. Gerry uses a certain eight-letter word to describe customers who don't pay on time, or ever. It's no wonder when we talk, the subject matter is mostly about these issues. There is, however, a discussion the two of us have that's worth noting. Once a year it happens, like clockwork.

Holiday time in my shop is typically slow. There's quite a bit of catering leading up to the last few weeks of the year, but after about mid-December, it's quiet until the first week of the New Year. Sometimes I wonder if we are the only people working during those weeks. Hours can pass without a phone call. It is, however, a good time to take a breath and look back on another year in business gone by. Everyone—customers, vendors and employees—tends to be in an upbeat mood. We look forward to this time to do all the things we missed during the year, like go out to lunch. I insist on having lunch served to me at least once during these weeks. One thing we can count on is a visit from Gerry. During the year he's in constant motion, but he makes a point to stop by around the holidays to drop off a gift of appreciation and catch up a little. We talk about work, family (Gerry is a devoted family man) and plans for the upcoming holidays. Soon enough the conversation changes. Although the wording might change a little from year to year, the subject is always the same. When are we going to retire from this business? Will either of us ever get a typical nine-to-five job?

"So, Pete, how many more years have you got?" Gerry asks.

"Not sure. My lease is almost up. Maybe it's time to sell the place and do something else? I don't know how much more of this I can take," I answer.

"How many years is it now?" he asks again.

"Twenty-four, I think. I lost count. How about you?" I ask.

"At least thirty. It's getting old. I still like the business. I just can't stand chasing around assholes for money anymore."

"I know what you mean," I say. "I've got one customer who is net 90 now. Can you believe it?"

"That's life I guess," Gerry says. "Do we really have a choice?"

"Maybe, maybe not. I don't know what else to do," I respond.

"Me neither," he agrees.

"So, see you next year?"

"Yeah, see you next year. Happy Holidays!"

Sure, it's not the most exciting interaction between the two of us, but it sums up our relationship perfectly. We have been working at our respective businesses a long time. It's a hard life, but it's even harder to imagine life without it. He's more than a vendor; in a life with few, I consider him a friend. Thanks, Gerry.

SICILIAN MUFFULETTA

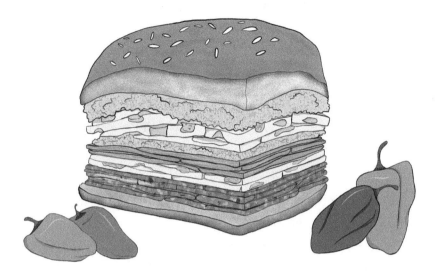

Like an Italian Combo, only bigger . . . and better!!

INGREDIENTS

1 10-inch muffuletta round bread (enough for 4 sandwiches)

1 pound Genoa salami

1 pound mortadella

¾ pound pepperoni

¾ pound sharp provolone cheese

¼ cup olive oil

2 T red vinegar

1 pound mixed assorted pitted olives

3-ounce container of giardiniera (pickled carrots, celery,
cauliflower) *(continued)*

(continued)

½ cup red roasted peppers

2 garlic cloves

Salt, pepper, and oregano

INSTRUCTIONS

In food processor, combine olive oil, red vinegar, olives, giardiniera, roasted peppers, garlic cloves, and a pinch of salt, pepper, and oregano. Pulse several times to form a spreadable tapenade. For stronger flavor, let sit in fridge for an hour or so.

Slice open bread and scoop out some of the dough. Generously spread layers of tapenade on both sides of the bread. Begin layering meats and cheese on bread. Start with Genoa salami then add mortadella and pepperoni. Layer provolone cheese on top of meats. Carefully close sandwich. Cut round bread into overstuffed quarters. Take a picture.

Plate and serve with Wise Sour Cream & Onion chips.

CHAPTER 16
BROWN-BAGGIN' IT

Remember how great it was to be a kid? No work, no major responsibilities, no mortgages! Those were the days. School, sports, and other activities filled our weeks. One could almost say being a kid is hedonistic. Life was about simple pleasures like best friends, pool parties, sleigh rides in the winter, and good times. Going to school was even fun. Everyone met at the bus stop and socialized before the big, yellow bus pulled around the corner. Its accordion-like door would open, and all of the neighborhood kids would head to school. Besides carrying books, most kids never forgot one important item: a brown-bag lunch. The brown-bag lunch has been a tradition for moms and kids for as long as there's been school. My mom was no exception. With a smile, she would hand me a bag filled with snacks, fruit, drinks, and always a sandwich, which I carried to school with pride and devoured at lunchtime. I have to admit, the sandwich didn't always make it to lunch. I'm sure I wasn't the only kid who sat in class and daydreamed about lunch, my favorite subject besides gym. I discovered when the teacher looked the other way it was my opportunity to grab a few bites of my sandwich. I often headed to lunch with a bag full of snacks only. School cafeteria food was completely unnecessary when armed with a bag lunch, except for pizza day, of course. Sitting at lunch we learned to barter for the first time. It was fun to watch everyone open their bags to display their wares. Trading chips and other treats occurred at every table. It was really a kid's version of high finance when nobody had any money. Even back then lunch was the best time of day. Yes, brown baggin' was, and still is, a way of life for school children, and it can't be beat. Adults, however, should visit their favorite sandwich shop for lunch at least a few days a week! Brown baggin', years later for us, also became a new technique of serving large corporate customers. We believe our small business, Gourmet Galley, has played an important role in bringing the brown-bag lunch to the corporate world. Way back in the early '90s, before ordering lunch became a technological chore requiring a computer or smartphone, we devised a way to deliver the brown-bag lunch to the office. It was an accident, actually. Here's what happened:

Back in 1993 when Mom, Dad, and I initially bought and took over Gourmet Galley in Greenwich, it was just a small restaurant and take-out spot. Deliveries were few and catering minimal. Greenwich is a busy little city just north of New York City, with numerous corporate parks and office complexes. There began a real emergence of companies, big and small, willing to, as a perk, provide lunch to their employees. As a well-known sandwich shop, we began circulating menus and marketing our services. It was easy at first. Companies were happy that they could call in or fax their orders to us. We would rapidly prepare the lunch orders and deliver them promptly. Lists would be sent to us as early as 9 a.m., with names of employees and their corresponding lunch of choice, usually handwritten, but sometimes typed. It reinforced what I had learned so many years ago: workers love lunchtime so much that they begin thinking about it first thing in the morning. Our job was to make the lunches and label them correctly. We would pack the entire lunch, soup, sandwiches, salads and drinks, in a box with the essentials and send it along with a delivery driver. We employed two drivers at the time, both driving a Gourmet Galley van, but eventually we needed more drivers. This process was fast, new, and exciting, as well as profitable. Month-end billing became the way to do business, as most companies opened house accounts. Very seldom did we receive cash payments.

One day Mom landed a new customer, a big trading firm with about fifty employees. They wanted to begin ordering lunch daily. An older woman, Catherine, worked in their kitchen. Her job was to collect the orders from all employees, write them on a piece of paper and fax it over around 10 a.m. The order was always a mess. Names scrawled here, there, and everywhere. Just deciphering it took ten minutes. We were thrilled to have the account, so we did the best we could. If she had add-ons, she would call. One day we had finished and sent the order, or at least that's what we thought. In a few minutes, the phone rang. It was Catherine. She said she was missing a BLT sandwich for one of the more impatient men on the list. (BLT is an extremely popular sandwich. People love bacon. I'm not sure if it's the crispy texture, the salty flavor, or the fact that it makes everything taste better. Some days it seems like we use more bacon than turkey!) I could see the BLT was crossed off the original order list. Even in the beginning we took pride in avoiding mistakes, especially with new customers. One of us assured her it was there. She told us she would double-check. Five minutes went by and another call, still no BLT. In fact, I could hear poor Catherine being harangued by someone in the background, presumably the man missing his BLT. On the phone an audible crash could be heard. "What was that?" I asked.

"Oh, nothing," she replied. "Sometimes the guys get so angry when their lunch doesn't arrive on time that they throw things at me. They usually miss though." It sounded like a splendid place to work. Regardless, I recalled making the sandwich and Mom recalled labeling it. It just had to be there. In order to rectify the situation, we made a new sandwich and sent it to her. At least she stopped calling. Later, at home after work, we discussed what had happened.

The three of us, Mom, Dad, and I, spent most of dinner discussing the mystery of the missing BLT. Our conclusion, after way too much discussion, was that someone at the company who forgot to order lunch took it. Simple crime: take a sandwich and eat it. Who will ever find out? We decided there must be a way to prevent lunch theft.

After considering several ideas that would never work, someone suggested the brown bag. We can take the order, complete it, and place each lunch in an individual brown bag. The bag will be labeled, using a black marker, with the corresponding person's name on the outside, and stapled to provide a little extra security. Lunch theft would become a thing of the past. Nobody would take a bag with someone else's name on it. It would be too easy to get caught.

The next day our brown-bag policy worked flawlessly. We soon implemented it with our large customers and some small ones, too. Everyone loved it, because it made distribution of lunches so easy. This system would become our contribution to corporate lunch delivery. We became the first restaurant in our area to deliver this way. The brown-bag system would be adopted by most of our competitors in the years to come.

A number of years later we began noticing changes in the lunch-ordering procedures. Companies began to create their own computer programs to simplify lunch. Employees would inform the person in charge of ordering what they wanted, and it was entered on a spreadsheet with all employee names printed, usually alphabetically. The sheet would be faxed over to restaurants and caterers like us. Upon receipt, scissors were used to cut the form. Each individual order had to be separated. As we finished orders and placed them in brown bags, we would staple the order sheets to each bag. It was similar to our original system, just a little easier to read the printed names on the bags. These systems were predecessors to online food ordering that was just around the corner and is so prevalent today. Some days it was common for us to go through hundreds of brown bags. It was a sight to see. In the back of our shop, ready to be delivered, were boxes with dozens of brown-bag lunches waiting for delivery. I always imagined, upon arrival, the smiles on the faces of the hungry recipients. It was, in a way, a tribute to the brown-bag lunch our moms used to give us. To think it started with a stolen BLT.

LIGHT–N–LIVELY

This is one of my favorite customer's favorite sandwiches. It's the ultimate BLT, and has been served in our place since day one.

INGREDIENTS

8 pieces white or wheat bread

4 lettuce leaves

1 sliced tomato

4 eggs

32 slices of bacon, or more depending on how much you like bacon!

1 small bunch chopped scallions

½ cup real mayonnaise

1 sliced avocado

(continued)

(continued)

INSTRUCTIONS

Place 4 eggs in boiling salted water. Remove in approximately 12 minutes. The eggs should be hard-boiled. Cool in cold running water and peel.

Cook bacon in oven set at 350 degrees. This should take 10 minutes or less. You can also cook bacon in a microwave. Times will vary. The bacon should be crispy.

Toast bread and mix scallions into mayonnaise.

Lay toasted bread on flat surface and spread scallion mayo on each slice. Place bacon on 4 slices of toast, about 8 slices on each. Layer lettuce leaves, sliced tomatoes and avocado on top of the bacon. Slice hard-boiled eggs and place one egg on each sandwich. Put top of bread on each and cut in half. For best taste, eat immediately.

Plate and serve with Deep River Zesty Jalapeño chips.

CHAPTER 17
THE GIRL OF MY DREAMS

There are so many things I enjoy about owning a family-run, busy sandwich shop. I enjoy the adrenaline rush of a busy lunch and the satisfaction we feel at the end of a good day. Most of all, though, what I like is the interaction I have with some great people day after day, customers especially. Over the past twenty-five years, we have operated Gourmet Galley at four separate addresses, and I can't recall one location with a paucity of great customers, real people like us, getting through the work week. Every day, starting at breakfast in early morning and continuing until the last few sandwiches are made at lunch, has been an opportunity to interact with hundreds of people. We have forged long-lasting relationships with all kinds of people; the diversity is staggering. We are the bartenders of lunch, only our elixir is the sandwich. A well-known jeweler at one point stopped by every morning for breakfast and conversation along with a teacher and his wife, a book editor. A successful mortgage broker became a close family friend after frequenting our shop and getting to know us. Another regular we know and love lives on his boat. We share lively conversation with him, though he often disappears for weeks at a time. He just sails away. Lawyers, stockbrokers, and executive assistants stop by for lunch at noon some days, while a little while later a construction or landscaping crew might wander in, exhausted from the morning's work, seeking sustenance and friendly conversation. The parade of customers who have graced our doors is an endless, fascinating variety of men and *women.*

As a twenty-something I figured it would be easy to meet, and possibly date, women who frequented the sandwich shop. I even thought I'd meet my future wife at the shop. It was easy to meet them, but dating was another story.

Dating customers never really occurred to me at first. With my mom standing five feet away and my dad ten feet away, having game was nearly impossible. Talk about awkward! But when it became clear that most of my social activity was taking place at work, I had to reconsider. With sandwich maker at the bottom of the list for men in demand, I needed a hook, something to break the ice. That was the easy part. If a woman I became friendly with over the counter seemed interested in me, I'd buy her a sandwich. That became my way of sparking some romance at the shop. I had some limited success. For instance, I dated a hairdresser briefly. Trading haircuts for sandwiches seemed like an even swap. When that relationship ran its course there were a few more. A stockbroker, a woman in retail, and another who worked in the employment business, all received, for a short time, the benefits of dating a sandwich maker—free lunch, or at least heavily discounted. As with many relationships, none of these developed beyond a handful of dates and nightly phone calls for a few weeks. My demanding lifestyle was simply not conducive to dating. To make matters worse, every time a relationship ended, it affected our bottom line; the ex would no longer frequent our establishment for lunch. Can you blame them? Again, awkward is an understatement. A cashier working for us during those years used to keep an eye out for the women I dated. (I never dated two at a time. Imagine the scene if, while dating two women, they came in for lunch at the same time? Who would I serve first, who gets a bigger discount, who do I talk to?) The cashier always took note if one of these women disappeared for a week or so, and she'd ask me what happened. I'd kind of look at her and we'd both have a laugh. Eventually, I decided it was no longer financially sound to date customers. Working seven days a week, from early to late, however, posed a major hurdle for me. How was I ever going to settle down? There were times when it seemed hopeless. I even recall trying a few blind dates. The good thing about working every day is it's a great excuse to get out of an uncomfortable blind date. I used that excuse many, many times, and it was never a lie. Luckily, in the late '80s early '90s, with the advent of the Internet, someone had a brilliant idea: Online dating sites. That is how I met my wife.

April 15, 2006. It's an easy day to remember because, of course, it is tax day. To me, other than tax day from yet another year, this date has major significance. It was a Saturday and the first date with my future wife. A few months earlier we had met on one of these new online dating sites. Before agreeing to meet we spent a little time communicating via email and realized we might actually like each other. We set up a time and place to meet in New York City and enjoyed lunch at a forgettable restaurant on the Upper West Side that probably isn't there anymore. Mei, as she likes to be called, ordered a Hawaiian Salad. I ordered a grilled chicken sandwich. It was a fairly disappointing selection. Not enough lettuce or tomato and the chicken serving was rather small. Sometimes I can't believe what some places pass off as sandwiches. I did not, however, complain. I was happy to get to know my date. Conversation was the norm for a first date. I had a feeling she'd expected a man a little taller and a little better looking, but she agreed to see me again, so I must have done something right. We planned to meet about a week later.

Mei, which sounds like the month, was born in Hong Kong but her family moved to Chinatown in New York City when she was very young. When we met she was living on Staten Island, having relocated a few years prior. Despite her change of borough, she still maintained excellent knowledge of landmarks, good eateries, and tea shops in Chinatown. She told me to meet her at a certain corner. I remember it was right under a statue of a noteworthy Chinese man, Confucius perhaps? I got there early and waited. I must have thought she was worth the wait because it was about an hour later when she finally arrived, very late. I even ate the snacks I had prepared for her, a few chocolate chip cookies and an apple. Being from the 'burbs I had no idea what life was like when you depend on public transportation.

She told me the bus had gotten stuck in traffic, but we could still grab a meal at a place just a few blocks away. Off we went down the street. We went to a Chinese restaurant, one like many we would frequent over the next several years. I was smart enough, and still am today, to let her do the ordering in Chinatown restaurants. Unfortunately, due to her tardiness, I had to cut the date short. There was something I had planned to do at work that day and it couldn't wait. I was impressed that Mei took no offense to my early departure. She really understood that I had work to do. The work of a self-employed sandwich shop/caterer, she learned, was never ending. This was a good sign, but it got better.

As the relationship blossomed the two of us spent more and more of our spare time together. As a teacher, Mei had weekends off. My weekends consisted of a few hours off here and there. The food business is relentless. So, we figured out a way to see each other and have a relationship despite my limited free time. Soon enough weekends were spent at my house. This meant plenty of time together, but it meant something else. Weekends have always been prep time for me. A few hours of prep on Saturday and Sunday assured an easier week at the shop. When we began spending weekends together I had to make that clear. Saturday and Sunday, though my business was closed, both included several hours of work. Not only was Mei okay with my working, she offered to help. I found out she actually wanted to help, and she proved a worthy assistant. So, the two of us would spend part of our time together in my shop prepping for the week to come. At lunchtime we would take a break and I would make sandwiches for us. Sometimes tuna or grilled chicken and sometimes a turkey combo with brie, lettuce, and tomato. The dressing was Mei's favorite, a basil pesto that I made, and still make, fresh every week. Pesto made with fresh basil, Parmesan cheese, pine nuts, salt, pepper, and olive oil is excellent with a fresh mozzarella and tomato salad, but really comes alive as a sandwich condiment.

Life was great as Mei and I were young-ish and in love. Sunday nights were spent driving back to Staten Island to drop Mei off at home. In the car we would complain about the long week ahead. Friday, when we would see each other again, seemed a long way off. I had to do something drastic as I couldn't let this one get away. I'd finally met an attractive, smart woman who actually understood my busy lifestyle. It would be a shame to let a little distance get in the way. I made a plan, executed and, with all the courage I could muster, on February 24, 2007, I asked her to marry me. It may have been a little corny, a giant fortune cookie with a proposal as the fortune, but I gave it my best shot. Luckily, she agreed. We set a date and were married later that year, in Hawaii.

Mei and I have celebrated over ten years of marriage by now and are still in love. Life may never be as fresh and new as those first few months of dating, but we still maintain a truly happy life with each other. Things are a bit more complicated, but what else should we expect with one daughter, three dogs and two turtles? Through all the years Mei has continued to be helpful and supportive of my lifestyle. She's been patient when I've needed to work late and has offered valuable creativity to menus and marketing campaigns. She's also provided me with plenty of moral support, a serious bonus for the self-employed. Life's a lot busier as well. Weekends are spent going here and there, rushing from one obligation to the next. It can be dizzying at times. Often, we reminisce how nice it was in the early days. Just the two of us falling in love, few distractions and few responsibilities. Life and love were so simple. How nice it was to be sitting together on a Sunday afternoon sharing a sandwich. Those are some of the fondest memories we have together.

FRESHER THAN FRESH [1,2]

Everyone loves pesto! When customers ask me for a recommendation from our menu, this one is my favorite choice.

INGREDIENTS

4 seeded semolina heroes

1½ pounds of sliced fresh roast turkey

1 head lettuce, chopped

1 large sliced tomato

1 pound sliced fresh mozzarella cheese

½ cup olive oil

½ cup grated Parmesan cheese

¼ cup pine nuts (you can substitute walnuts)

2 cups fresh basil leaves

1½ cups baby spinach (baby spinach will give the pesto a
  bright green color)
1 garlic clove (you don't want the garlic to overpower the fresh basil)
Salt and pepper

INSTRUCTIONS

In food processor mix Parmesan cheese, pine nuts, a pinch of salt and pepper, basil leaves and garlic. Add a little olive oil and turn on food processor. As ingredients begin to mix add more olive oil. Begin to add baby spinach a handful at a time. The pesto is done when all ingredients are blended well. Some oil might rise to the top, but otherwise, it should not be oily.

Slice open semolina heroes and lay flat. Spread pesto on top and bottom of all 4 heroes.

On bottom half of the hero layer chopped lettuce and tomatoes followed by the fresh mozzarella slices. Layer generous amounts of fresh roast turkey over the cheese on each and put top half of hero on each sandwich. Cut in half.

Plate and serve with Lay's Limón potato chips.

CHAPTER 18

"ONLY BAD THINGS CAN HAPPEN"

When Dad heard the news he shook his head. None of us knew how to react, but, with his signature negativity, he made a statement that is repeated over and over in our family. We had found out that Allie, my younger sister, was dating Santiago, at that time an employee of ours. Allie is a native of Colombia and was adopted by my mom when her three biological children had all grown up. "Grown up" for me means I had simply gotten older!

Dad remarked, "Only bad things can happen from this relationship." He walked around muttering how soon enough she would be pregnant and single—very optimistic.

I don't think any of us either agreed or disagreed, we simply accepted it and worried. We had no idea where the relationship was headed. It began in the year 2001 and, as of today, has resulted in a marriage, a business partner, and three grandchildren for my parents. I never imagined it would turn out this way and I can probably speak for Mom and Dad, too. Who would have thought that one of my sisters would have dated and ended up marrying one of our employees? I give more credit to Santiago than Allie; he's had to put up with the entire Roseman family over the years. I guess falling in love affects everyone differently. It's quite a story.

Santiago was born in Brazil but became a U.S. citizen some time ago. His name is pronounced just as it's spelled, S-A-N-T-I-A-G-O. It's not any of the following: Sammy, Sam, Samuel, or, even S. I've even heard him called Diego a few times. Santi is about the most acceptable way to shorten his name as far as I'm concerned. Santiago is also the name of Chile's capital city, and it's not that difficult to pronounce. I suppose he's used to having his name mangled. Anyway, during his early years in the States he lived with his older sister, Sarah, in Port Chester, New York. He spent most of his time at school or work. At one point, after finishing school, he accepted a job at a local restaurant. With his friendly, accommodating personality he was a natural with customers and enjoyed the work. The year was 2000. Coincidentally, at that time our business was desperately searching for a new location. Our landlord had plans for his building that did not include our shop, so we had two choices: find a suitable location or close. Luckily, we were approached by a restaurateur in need of management assistance for his struggling restaurant, which also specialized in sandwiches. It seemed like a good fit, our catering and take-out and his restaurant, so we merged operations. This was the first time we moved locations. The restaurant was just around the corner, so the move was easy and fast, done over one weekend. We were able to maintain our name, Gourmet Galley, in hopes of reducing confusion among our vast corporate customer list. That was about all we maintained. Nothing was easy after that! The restaurant was enormous, with two floors, a huge kitchen in the basement and a long, vast dining room upstairs. There was even a dumbwaiter to bring trays up and down more efficiently. It broke constantly so we relied primarily on each other. To say it was a difficult work atmosphere is an understatement. Maintaining this large restaurant as well as our catering proved nearly impossible. Taking on a partner became the worst and best thing we did in twenty-five years of business. The worst, because from the first day it was destined to fail, for too many reasons. To this day I don't think our partner, named Mark, even told any of his employees about the change. We kind of just showed up one Saturday in October. It was all too complicated. The best, because Santiago was working at that restaurant and came along with the partnership. There were days when it seemed he and I managed the entire restaurant ourselves, about thirty tables! I would run downstairs and grab as many plates as humanly possible. At the top of the stairs, Santiago would take them from me and distribute according to the orders. I'm sure there were times when we made mistakes, but it was so busy that customers were probably too scared to interrupt us. Of course, we did not know the end result at the time, but right away, he proved to be a smart, hard-working, loyal employee. An employee like this is invaluable in the restaurant world. Customers and employees liked Santiago. So did Allie. Soon enough they were dating.

The restaurant partnership ended after less than two years and we were forced to move our shop to a new location. This was our second move and third spot in the town of Greenwich. We set up shop a few blocks away from the restaurant in a much smaller space with no restaurant seating. The year was 2002 and the operation simplified. Santiago came along as an employee, helped set up the new spot, and became a fixture at the shop. The one thing that stood out to us was his dedication. Long hours, extra work, whatever the job entailed he was enthusiastic and happy to help. He also became an excellent sandwich maker! While dating Allie he got to know the business well, and in 2006, they married, so in 2008, when we were again forced to move, this time to our fourth location, we took the next logical step. As my parents' roles were diminishing, we offered Santiago a partnership. He didn't know at the time that a partnership in a small business such as ours basically means more work, more worry, and more hours for similar compensation. Welcome to my world! The two of us opened the shop in Stamford, just about ten minutes north of Greenwich. The rest, as they say, is history.

It's been over eighteen years now since we first met Santiago. As of now the two of us run the day-to-day operations of our sandwich shop in Stamford. He is still a natural with customers. He skillfully manages the phone, computer, and walk-in customers at the same time, without ever a hint of impatience. I marvel at his ability to perform these tasks adroitly, as I've been known to be a little terse when overwhelmed. I think Santiago probably makes fun of me when I'm in the back! We've spent the last ten years in the same location so have found a fairly permanent home. Mom and Dad still work, though a bit less. Our sandwich shop is truly a family business. Customers laugh when I tell them we are brothers. We are brothers-in-law, of course, but he is also one of the few people I've ever known whom I trust completely. His concern for the well-being of those around him is atypical. One time, before I knew him well, I was forced to spend the weekend in a local hospital. My mom and dad were both sick as well. On Sunday, after I was released, I wasn't sure how I'd get home. Santiago appeared out of nowhere to give me a ride. It was a kind gesture I never forgot. We joke once in a while that I'd still be at the hospital today if it was not for his assistance.

Over the years Santiago has proven to be an honest, trustworthy partner and a good friend. To replace him would be nearly impossible. Outside of work, Allie and Santiago have endured the years well. They have three children, Lucas, Nina, and Julian. Santiago handles my sister with the same skill and dexterity that has proven so valuable at work. Sometimes I'm sure it's not so easy. We often celebrate holidays, birthdays, and special occasions together. As an in-law and business partner he's as good as it gets. Mom and Dad would agree wholeheartedly (though Dad might be slower to admit he might have prejudged the relationship!). Looking back over the years, it's hard to believe everything we've been through. We've enjoyed the good times and endured the not so good times. There have been triumphs and laughter as well as a few disappointments. He has handled the disappointments better than I. Through it all, Santiago has remained steadfast. It is amazing things turned out like this. If, according to Dad, these are "bad things," I'll take them any day.

BRAZILIAN BAURU

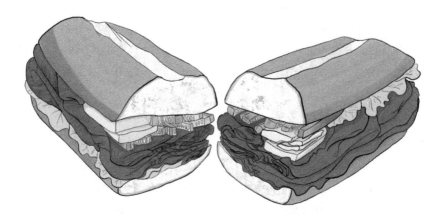

A classic from South America. The melted cheese tastes so good, the sandwich doesn't need dressing.

INGREDIENTS

4 French rolls

1½ pounds of rare roast beef

¼ pound sliced mozzarella cheese

1 large sliced beefsteak tomato

½ cup dill pickle slices

½ tsp. oregano

Salt

INSTRUCTIONS

Preheat oven to 350 degrees.

Slice open French rolls and lay flat. Place one slice of mozzarella cheese on each side of the 4 rolls. Place rolls on baking sheet and put in the oven. In about 5 minutes remove the rolls. The cheese should be melted and gooey.

Layer roast beef on each of the 4 roll bottoms followed by tomatoes and pickle slices. Sprinkle oregano and salt on each sandwich before placing other half of roll on top. Cut in half.

Plate and serve with Lay's Cheddar and Sour Cream chips.

CHAPTER 19
5,000 SANDWICHES

We got a call in the spring of 1998. There was an upcoming classic car show being held in town over a May weekend and a local businessman was interested in hiring a caterer along with showing his fancy cars. Why would he need a caterer? He wanted to meet with us. There were no additional details revealed. His assistant set up a meeting so, late in the afternoon one day, Mom and Dad drove to his office down the street. The mysterious catering job would be revealed, and it was quite a shock.

The businessman owned several car dealerships in town and planned to have a tent set up at the car show. As a marketing gimmick he wanted to give out free lunch. He imagined anyone and everyone who would attend the car show might get hungry. What better way to create a buzz than by giving away free lunch? The show expected thousands of people over a two-day period so that meant thousands of potential car-buying customers. Fancy yellow bags with the dealership name printed on the side were made just for the occasion. In the bags would go a package of chips, a water, a twin-pack chocolate chip cookie, and, of course, a sandwich. To keep it simple it would be ham or turkey and cheese with lettuce on a roll, mustard and mayo packets on the side. Here's where we came in. The order was for 5,000 sandwiches, to be prepared and handed out by us on Saturday and Sunday during the car show.

The first thing we had to do was figure out if the plan was feasible. Could our small operation handle this huge task? After a brief analysis, we decided to go for it. What a great opportunity. No way we could turn down this challenge. We enthusiastically began preparing for the event, which was just a few weeks away. Vendors were alerted, and our crew was ready to take on this enormous endeavor. Aside from Mom, Dad, and I we had quite the group. There was Carlos, a natural workhorse who could bang out sandwiches faster than just about anyone I'd met. There was also Jose, maybe the hardest worker to come out of Guatemala. He simply never stopped working. In all the years he worked for us he insisted on working until the very last minute of his shift, and was happy to work more if necessary. Also, there was Antonio, an older, comical man from Guatemala as well, who kept us laughing with his broken English and crazy habits. He'd walk around with a cabbage leaf on his head or pretend kitchen items were coming out of certain bodily orifices. Very mature. Last, there was Servi, a young man from one of the Central American countries, who would do just about anything we asked with a big smile and great attitude. This crew was in charge not only of making the sandwiches, but also working the tent at the car show giving the bag lunches to hungry attendees. Though we were confident as the event date approached, deep inside there was still the burning question: Could we really make 5,000 sandwiches in such a short amount of time? We would find out.

The Friday before the show arrived and it was business as usual at Gourmet Galley until after lunch. We decided to close early and begin the job. We officially commenced making sandwiches at 4 p.m., Friday afternoon. The plan was to split the sandwich making between Friday and Saturday nights. As we began, everyone staked their own space in the kitchen and started to work. Carlos grabbed a large spot up in front while Jose chose a small corner in the back of the kitchen. Our kitchen was small at the time, an L shape with three exclusive work stations that became six work stations that weekend. Antonio worked next to Jose and, in the middle of it all, I worked at my own station. My mom was able to work next to Carlos, and my dad kind of walked around and worried. Boxes of rolls were stacked to the ceiling. Lettuce had been chopped and filled a new, clean 55-gallon container. Servi, in charge of slicing turkey and ham, stationed himself next to the automatic slicer we had rented for the job, his home for the next two days. Turkey, ham, and cheese filled the kitchen. Piles and piles of ham and turkey were stacked in every station. Servi also was in charge of opening the plastic pre-packaged sliced American cheese. It seemed every few seconds he was tearing into a new sleeve. All of us tried to work neatly but it was impossible, there was just too much work to worry about cleaning. There was light conversation but mostly we kept our heads down. Knives sliced sandwiches in half and the sandwiches were then wrapped in deli paper. Boxes of deli paper were set up in each station. The goal was not to make fancy sandwiches; the goal was to make sandwiches as fast as possible. That's what we did! We boxed sandwiches by the hundreds. The boxes were then labeled and stuffed into a refrigerated truck parked out back. By 9 o'clock the crew had about 1,500 sandwiches complete. By midnight we'd done 3,000. Time to go home and sleep. Tomorrow, Saturday, the car show would open. None of us knew what to expect.

The crew arrived at the event location by 9 a.m. It was a municipal park by the Long Island Sound, a perfect place for a car show. We watched as cars pulled into the show—some were driven but the fancier cars were towed. There would be time to check out the show later, we thought. Carlos got busy setting up a station on the front tables under the tent. The truck with the sandwiches backed up near the tent, which had been set up the night before. Chips, cookies, and waters were stacked on tables that were set up in back of the tent. Jose and Antonio, unaware of how the next few hours would unfold, began unpacking the labeled, fancy lunch bags. They figured a few stacks here and there would be fine. As the sun rose so did the temperature. It would be a hot one. At about 11:30 a few people trickled in and asked what we were doing.

"Free lunch?" someone asked, almost kidding.

"Yes, actually," I answered. "As much as you want. Ham or turkey sand-wiches."

We had strict instructions. Absolutely no limit on quantities. Whatever people wanted they were to receive. Then the fun began. The line started as a trickle but quickly gained steam and grew. It was as if someone had told a friend at the show about the free lunch and news spread like wildfire and this was way before Twitter! From all directions at the event they began descending on our small tent. If lunch was to be given out for free, nobody wanted to miss it. For my crew, in our small tent, there was nowhere to hide. The line began and got longer and longer. People were loving it. Carlos would address an approaching person and offer turkey or ham.

"I'll take two turkeys," someone would say.

"Two turkeys," he'd yell back to Jose. Jose would drop two turkey sandwiches in bags with the appropriate items to finish it off. Carlos would grab the bags and hand them to another happy customer. As things got moving people began asking for more, three, four, five, even ten sandwiches at a time. I saw a family of five ask for twenty bags. Planning the next few days of meals I guessed. Servi and I were running back and forth to the truck reloading sandwiches as fast as we could. Jose and Antonio struggled mightily to keep up. It was a matter of survival. Once in a while we'd look up to see the line of people, like a snake, stretched out hundreds of feet as far as we could see, people happily waiting patiently for free lunch. We wondered when it would slow down. As the day progressed, the line never stopped. It was clear to us the sandwiches, not the cars, were becoming the main attraction of the show. That must have been the goal all along. All day we were bombarded by the car show attendees, I think some of them must have come back for seconds . . . and thirds. What's better than free lunch? Free lunch and dinner! As the afternoon wore on our little tent looked like a war zone of sandwiches. We were guzzling water bottles and eating chips just to keep up with the heat. Boxes, wrappers, empty bottles, and excess clothing littered the area. At one point, my dad stopped by to see how things were going. I looked at him and rolled my eyes. He may as well have gone to the end of the line to wait for a sandwich. It was quite a scene, and there was still one more day and 2,000 more sandwiches to go.

We cleaned up and headed back to the shop for another night of sandwiches. Everyone was exhausted, but no one would admit it. The whole crew, Mom, Dad, Me, Carlos, Jose, Antonio, and Servi, put our heads down and got the sandwiches done early Saturday night. The light atmosphere from the night before was gone. We worked in total silence. All of us needed a good night's sleep. The following day would be the final day of the sandwich, I mean "car" show.

Sunday proved to be just as hot and just as busy. The line for free lunch began mid-morning and continued until the event began to wind down at around 5 p.m. It was like all the people from the day before returned and brought a friend. As things eased up towards the end we got to walk around the car show a bit. It was funny because when we heard people talking, invariably, it wasn't so much about the cars, but more about that great free lunch they got. Mission accomplished for the businessman who had hired us. He'd managed to make the entire car show about the free lunch. Back at the tent we finally sat down, completely spent. At the same time a real sense of accomplishment came over all of us. There, in our sweat-soaked T-shirts and filthy shoes, we kind of looked at each other. Since Friday afternoon we'd logged countless hours of work and had answered the burning question. We'd made and given out 5,000 sandwiches. The car show ended, and everyone headed home. All that was left from our tent was a few boxes of bags and some leftover bottled water. Every morsel of food was gone, given away. Our crew headed out for a well-deserved beer. Mom, Dad, and I got in our car and drove home. We were all tired, too tired to have a conversation. It was a relief to be done with the biggest catering job we ever had. It was quite a weekend, but tomorrow would be Monday, back to business. At one point my dad asked, "Do you think we could have done 10,000?"

MONTE CRISTO[14]

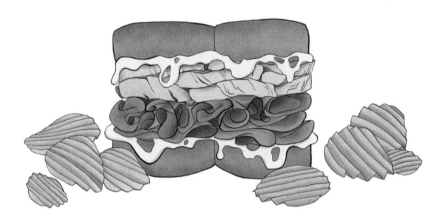

There are a variety of ways to make this delicious hot sandwich. I prefer the turkey and ham combo. Best made with challah. Try berry jam on the side for dipping!

INGREDIENTS

8 slices challah

6 eggs, beaten

¾ pound sliced turkey breast

¾ pound sliced boiled ham

¼ pound Swiss or Gruyère cheese

¼ cup real mayonnaise

¼ cup Dijon mustard

½ stick unsalted butter

(continued)

(continued)

    Powdered sugar (optional)

    Favorite berry jam (optional)

INSTRUCTIONS

Lay challah on flat surface and spread mayonnaise on 4 slices and mustard on the other four slices. Place a slice of cheese on each piece of challah. Layer turkey and ham on the challah slice spread with mayo and place each slice with mustard on top to complete sandwiches.

Heat frying pan to medium. Melt enough butter to cover entire pan. Dip sandwiches, one at a time, in the eggs, coating each side. Place one sandwich in the middle of the frying pan and cook until golden brown on bottom. Flip and cook the other side of the sandwich. If you have a grill press now is a good time to use it. It will help in melting the cheese.

Repeat step 2 until all sandwiches are complete. Dust the top of each with a sprinkle of powdered sugar and cut each sandwich in half. Spoon berry jam into bowl.

Plate and serve with Deep River New York Spicy Dill Pickle chips.

CHAPTER 20
HERE'S THE (ROAST) BEEF

Over the last few decades in the food service business I've acquired many skills. I can de-bone chicken breast, make lasagna like a real Italian (I'm not!), and make any number of tasty soups from split pea to chicken noodle. I can tell when refrigeration isn't working properly, without a thermometer, and know exactly when a grease trap needs cleaning. I make tuna salad, several kinds of chicken salad, and egg salad as well as the creamiest, dreamiest coleslaw on the east coast. Yes, when it comes to deli fare I've mastered quite a bit since I began.

But there's one skill that stands out that I learned in our early years, when my family owned the meat market and catering business in upstate Connecticut, the market that didn't work out for us.

Customers have always asked why my roast beef tastes so good and I smile. I was taught to trim, tie and cook my own roast beef by a real old-fashioned butcher at that shop. It's a skill that has provided Gourmet Galley with delicious roast beef sandwiches time after time. The roast beef I make is medium rare, cooked three hours, and is the most delectable you can find. It's tender, juicy, and oh so flavorful. The taste far exceeds prepackaged brands. During the first years of my marriage I'd call my wife to tell her I was running late. She would answer the phone and say, "Roast beef, again?" Making my own roast beef has always been an after-hours task when the kitchen is dark and quiet. The taste and quality, however, are worth it.

In our initial, however brief, foray in the food service business, Mom, Dad, and I struggled mightily with the meat market/deli/catering combo that proved so difficult to manage. It was a valuable learning experience for all of us, however, and paid huge dividends down the road when we took over Gourmet Galley, the sandwich shop that would occupy our lives. I was young, just out of college, and eager to learn. I tried to learn every aspect of the business as fast as possible. One day I'd work in the deli, while the next I'd spend on the meat counter or in the busy kitchen. I was high energy, all over the place. I remember the meat department was a little intimidating. The meat-cutting room was cold, with a walk-in cooler nearby that was even colder. In the walk-in was the largest meat grinder I'd ever seen. It looked like you could fit an entire person in there. Sharp knives were everywhere and there was always a huge bucket full of beef and pork fat. I learned early that once a week a pig farmer stopped by to load up the fat, to be used as feed for his pigs. There was also this evil-looking band saw. It was huge and looked like it could cut through anything. It stood over six feet tall and resembled a giant, upright chainsaw. Loud and sharp, it screamed, "Stay away from me!" when turned on. I noticed some of the old-school butchers hadn't heeded this warning. Let's just say some of them did not have all ten complete digits! Just watching the machine in action made me cringe at first, though eventually I learned how to use it and I still have all of my fingers! That room is where I worked with an old-time butcher named Bob, who must have been around seventy years old when I knew him. He took it upon himself to train me. It was with Bob that I learned how to make a truly great roast beef.

Bob was like a big teddy bear. Tall with wide shoulders and a set of paws on him like I'd never seen. Years of working as a butcher had left an indelible imprint on those hands. Calloused and rough, his hands reflected a lifetime of hard work. I wondered to myself if my hands would ever look like that. Not as of yet; however I do have plenty of work-related scars, ailments, aches, and pains. Bob was a proud veteran but talked very little of his time in the military. I'd ask him a question like, "How long did you serve and where?"

Instead of answering the question, he would reply, "You know how we kept ourselves occupied in the service?" I'd look at him and shake my head.

"Wine, woman, and song," he'd smile, and we'd move along. The older Italian female customers loved good old Bob. Sometimes a particular woman, noticing him in the meat room, would demand he come out to the meat counter and help as she chose her roasts, chicken cutlets, and chopped meat. "She's an old family friend," he'd always tell me, "I've been waiting on her for years."

One day he told me I was going to learn how to make roast beef, the right way. He directed me to go into the walk-in cooler and take out two top inside rounds, the cut of beef I still use today. This cut makes perfect roast beef. It's a tender cut and it's easy to slice on the meat slicer. After trimming, and before cooking, it's nice to cut one large two-inch steak off the end. The sliced steak is called top round London broil. It can be marinated and cooked on a grill or in a broiler. Cut into thin slices it's great for stir fry or stroganoff.

Bob and I stood side-by-side at the work table. He towered over me and pushed and pulled the twenty-five-pound piece of meat like it weighed nothing. His skill with the knife was remarkable, with speed and accuracy from years working in a butcher shop. I struggled to keep up. He showed me exactly where to find "seams" in the meat where trim—extra meat— would easily tear away. The trim, he explained, could be used to make chopped meat. He worked quickly and efficiently while he showed me. He told me to keep a thin layer of fat on top to enhance the flavor. Finally, Bob took a roll of twine and informed me that the meat needed to be tied at least twice, with the grain. This would ensure even cooking. That day he taught me the meat cutter's knot as well and, soon enough, we had two roast beefs trimmed and tied, ready for the oven. I fumbled with the string for a while, but eventually mastered it. All they needed was a little garlic and pepper on top before being cooked for about three hours at 350 degrees.

Bob turned to me and said, "You think you got it?"

With a bit of bravado I said, "Sure, no problem."

III

"Do 1,000 of them, then you'll be an expert like me," Bob replied as he walked out of the meat room to tend to a customer. After this lesson, I would show up to work early and practice my new skill. When Bob arrived later and saw a couple of prepped roast beefs on the counter he smiled. "Did I do those last night?" he'd ask, smiling at me.

It's been more than twenty-five years since I first learned to trim, tie, and cook my own roast beef. Since then I think I've bought prepackaged roast beef only about a half dozen times. If I had to guess how many I've trimmed, tied, and cooked, I'd say probably more than five thousand. Over five thousand roast beefs used to make delicious, rare roast beef sandwiches with mayo, Russian dressing, or horseradish sauce. Sliced and chopped on the grill, the roast beef makes juicy steak-and-cheese sandwiches, with favorites such as fried onions, peppers, and mushrooms added. Bite after bite, the roast beef I've prepared has been a staple on our menus and a customer favorite. The extra trim from the beef is never wasted. I use a meat grinder to make lean, fresh ground meat. With the ground meat, I've made burritos, quesadillas, and tons of chili. Just the right amount of heat, ground beef mixed with kidney beans and assorted seasoning makes chili that sticks to your ribs and is great on a cold day.

Roast beef I could always call my own, cooked medium rare just right almost every time, is the result of my hard work. I love cooking it on a weekday morning. The aroma fills the shop. Customers who walk in invariably comment on how good it smells. The tempting aroma usually leads to an easy lunch decision: a roast beef sandwich. Once or twice I have made the mistake of attempting to cook it at night. I planned to go home and return in three hours. Unfortunately, I often would forgot about it, and arrive in the morning to find roast beef that resembles shoe leather. Oy! That aside, learning this skill has been a real benefit. When a customer comes in and asks how the roast beef looks, I think back to those early days in the cold meat room. Bob has probably passed on by now, but I still give him a little credit for every roast beef I make. I describe the beef as "Outstanding!" I then suggest a sandwich with coleslaw and Russian dressing or another with lettuce, tomatoes, pickles and mayo, two classic combos, very hard to resist. My hands may never resemble the immense, powerful paws that Bob used so skillfully in the meat-cutting room, but he'd be proud of me anyway.

LA VACHE

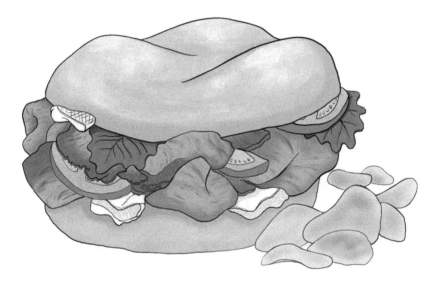

In French this word means cow. This sandwich has been a staple on our menu for many years and is amazing when the bread is fresh and the roast beef is medium rare.

INGREDIENTS

4 club rolls
1½ pounds sliced rare roast beef
½ pound brie cheese   *(continued)*

(continued)

    1 large sliced tomato

    4 lettuce leaves

    1 small slice red onion

    ½ cup real mayonnaise

    2 T horseradish (water squeezed out)

INSTRUCTIONS

In mixing bowl, combine mayonnaise and horseradish until well blended.

Slice open club rolls lengthwise and generously spread with horseradish dressing.

Layer lettuce leaves, tomatoes, and onions on club roll followed by thinly-sliced brie cheese.

Layer roast beef on top and close club roll. Cut in half.

Plate and serve with Boulder Canyon Sweet Vidalia Onion chips.

CHAPTER 21
DOGS DAY AFTERNOON

The year 2008 was a good year for canines in the Roseman household. Early in my marriage to Mei we decided it would be nice to have a dog. At the time she had a dog, Lucky. He was an overprotective, highly possessive, 125-pound boxer-bull mix who, for some reason, never warmed up to me. I guess he figured out what was going on and decided that whoever this guy was who took his owner (Mei) away every week was no friend of his. This made it impossible for us to take Lucky to my house in Connecticut, so he remained with Mei's sister, Kerry. After careful consideration we decided a rescue dog would be best for us. Having visited several shelters in our area, we realized that so many abandoned dogs needed homes. It felt like the right thing to do. One January day in 2008, we headed over to an animal shelter in Mamaroneck, New York.

Upon entering the shelter, we were welcomed with incessant, loud barking of about two dozen dogs, mostly pit bulls. It wasn't the welcome we expected. The woman behind the desk warned us that if we were looking for a small, cute designer dog, we were in the wrong place. She pointed to the back and said we should take a look, if we dared. Before heading towards the barking my wife noticed a female black dog, alone in a cage separate from the rest of the shelter dogs. She asked the woman about the dog, who seemed very sad and emaciated, but had this shiny black coat and deep-set dark eyes. Someone had dropped her off, the woman said, and the poor dog had been on a hunger strike ever since. The woman wasn't sure if the dog was going to survive. Currently, the dog was on medication to make her eat. We decided to take her for a walk.

As soon as we got out of the shelter the beautiful black dog came alive. Tail wagging, jumping up and down, she seemed very happy to be with us. Easy decision. We named her Maggie and took her home. Soon after we took her home Maggie began to eat, play, and enjoy being a dog again. The one thing I always noticed was that she truly appreciated us being with her. When we took her in the back yard she had this way of looking back to make sure we were coming along when heading outside. She even began to learn commands and would come racing back to me when I beckoned. At night I would watch television and Maggie would put her head in my lap and fall asleep. Soon, this once emaciated forty-pound pooch grew into a ninety-pound house protector. Truthfully though, her bark has always been worse than her bite. One day, about four months later, Mei and I realized that Maggie had too much alone time. We were both at work during the day, so it was obvious what we had to do.

On a Monday in April, we headed to another animal shelter, this one in Elmsford. When we got there, we could not believe what we saw. There were dogs everywhere. The small shelter was overrun by animals. Every inch of space was used to stack cages for the hundreds of dogs and cats on the premises. There were also dozens of dogs roaming free. I guess the shelter ran out of cages or just gave up. They assured us that any animals roaming free were friendly. All of the sudden we saw this little beagle standing on a desk. He had this adorable little howl. I think he also lifted his leg and peed on the desk, a precursor of life with an untrainable, stubborn beagle! Mei asked one of the women in charge if he was available, and luckily, he was. Without hesitation we adopted him, named him Beau, and brought him home to meet Maggie. They liked each other right away. The only problem was Maggie outweighed Beau by about fifty pounds. Her favorite game became running at full speed and knocking him over. It was a sight to see as poor little Beau would roll over a few times, get up, shake it off and proceed to run away from Maggie. A few months later, Mei decided Beau could use a friend closer in size. Perhaps they could team up on Maggie?

In August of that year we found a beagle rescue group in Ventnor City, New Jersey, at least two hours away from our home in Stamford. The woman who headed the group had a litter of beagle puppies and offered us one to adopt. My wife and I got into the car on a Saturday afternoon and drove almost three hours to be greeted by a playpen full of beagle puppies. It was difficult to choose one, but, finally, we settled on the one most similar to Beau, a female we named Belle. She was just a few weeks old when we got her, and fit in the palm of our hand. We drove home and introduced Belle to Beau and Maggie. She was feisty and made it clear early on she would not be pushed around. In less than eight months we went from zero to three dogs. That's a lot of dog poop. We kept a major supply of plastic bags around and still do. All three rescue puppies became quite a commitment. Our house was bursting with energy. It must have been a sight for our neighbors to see the five of us heading down the street.

Having three dogs around can be challenging. Eating a meal can be a difficult task. I am a huge pushover when it comes to feeding them. It's obvious to me that whatever humans eat is far superior to what dog food must taste like. I feel obligated to share whatever I eat with the three of them, whether it's chicken, cheese, salmon, or, of course, sandwiches. Saturday lunch is a weekly treat for all of us. No rushing or pressure, just an enjoyable meal at home. I like to eat tuna or chicken salad on the weekends, especially open face on a bagel. Sweet curried chicken salad, with raisins and mango chutney on a bagel, along with a bag of chips, is a great Saturday lunch. Our three dogs will sit at attention while lunch is prepared. As the sandwiches are brought to the table, Maggie usually sits underneath the table and the other two, Beau and Belle, will sit on either side of my seat. They anxiously await the treats I will soon be sharing. First, I'll give each of them some bread by breaking off small pieces here and there. Soon enough I'll be tossing chips in the air as the three of them jump up to catch them in midair. They munch and crunch with such joy as they help me finish off my sandwich. I appreciate their different personalities on display, especially at mealtime. Often, after lunch, the four of us will catch a short nap on the couch before the afternoon activities begin with my wife and daughter.

Until I had dogs I never appreciated them as pets. Having four-legged friends greet you after a hard day's work is a great way to be welcomed home. They don't care how your day was or even if you are a few minutes late. They are just happy to see you, and, to this day, upon arriving home, I hear the calls of Maggie, Beau, and Belle. Maggie barks, Beau whines, and Belle yaps like a puppy. As I enter, the three of them are at the foot of the stairs waiting for my attention. Sometimes I think they are happier to see me than are my wife and daughter. After taking the dogs out back to run around we head inside. Eventually they settle down. At night, after dinner, the three of them like to keep me company while I read, watch television, or finish work on the computer. They seem happiest when we are on the couch. I'll sit in the middle and they will jockey for a chance to lay their heads on my lap. It's so relaxing and makes me happy too. They are truly this man's best friend.

Author's note: Unfortunately, during the writing of this book I was forced to put down our youngest dog, Belle. She had an incurable heart condition.

THE ROSEMAN DOGS

OPEN-FACE CURRIED CHICKEN SALAD[19]

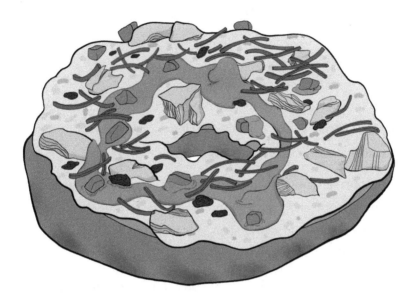

At Gourmet Galley we sell more curried chicken salad than traditional chicken salad. Sweet with juicy raisins and a mango chutney, it just can't be beat.

INGREDIENTS

4 bagels, any flavor except cinnamon raisin

3-4 pounds raw boneless chicken breast (white meat turkey can be used as a substitute)

1 cup black raisins

1 cup shredded carrots

1–1½ cups mayo (depending on how much mayo you like in
    chicken salad)   *(continued)*

(continued)

½ cup mango chutney

2 T curry powder

Salt and pepper

Lettuce leaves and thinly sliced cucumber (optional)

INSTRUCTIONS

In a double boiler steam chicken breast until internal temperature reaches 165 degrees. Let cool and chop into ½-inch cubes. I prefer not to boil chicken directly in water; it retains too much.

In mixing bowl combine chicken, raisins, carrots, mango chutney, curry powder, salt and pepper and mix well. The mixture should be yellow and slightly wet from mango chutney. Add mayo and mix again. The curried chicken salad is now complete.

Slice open bagels and lay flat. Spread a thin layer on both sides of each bagel. Do not close bagels.

As an alternative, place lettuce leaves on bagels first, then chicken salad, and top off with sliced cucumbers.

Plate and serve with Cape Cod Sea Salt chips.

CHAPTER 22
GUAPO

Years ago we had an employee named Antonio, a short, wiry man from Guatemala with an insane work ethic and bizarre sense of humor. He kept everyone in the kitchen laughing with his everyday antics, either on purpose or by accident. He is the same Antonio who helped us make 5,000 sandwiches one weekend. Dad and Antonio had a "special" relationship. They would go on deliveries together and race up and down the stairs. Their jokes revolved around the human excretory system. The bond was genuine with only a few problems. First of all, Antonio's main language was a dialect from back country Guatemala. He could not read or write English, but made us laugh when he pretended. As we scanned a lunch order he would stand next to us, nodding in agreement. Also, Antonio could never pronounce Dad's name properly. Bless his heart for trying, but I never heard anyone butcher the name "Herb" as bad as he. So, he improvised. Antonio decided to come up with a nickname for Dad: "Guapo." It means "the handsome one," according to his version of the Spanish language. Everyone smiled when he began to call Dad "Guapo" and, after more than twenty years, the nickname has stuck among our employees.

Guapo has been the most important behind-the-scenes person in our business since the beginning. He made it abundantly clear from the start that he was a numbers guy. His prowess was not with food preparation or service—though he was never shy about lending a hand—but with keeping the books in order and instilling a work ethic in us that we never thought we had. Despite not being a foodie, he actually helped create the Mexicali Rose burrito, one of our most popular menu items. No, he has never met a bagel he couldn't cut, and he brews a mean pot of coffee, but he isn't about to start grilling chicken or making soup. Instead, he has tirelessly shown up day after day, year after year, a model of consistency worthy of emulation. There's a sort of distinguished elegance to his work ethic, a real everyman who has provided staunch support at each and every turn over the years. Who else would have processed nearly 50,000 invoices, hundreds of month-end billings, tax returns for each year, and numerous other thankless tasks? Tasks that, though sometimes loathsome, must be completed with regularity for the success of a small business. He has been truly invaluable.

I remember the early years when our small business started to grow. Dad and I would wake up at 3:45 a.m. and get ready for work. We lived together at first. Due to the hours we put in, sometimes eighty a week, it made sense. There were plenty of mornings when I could easily have stayed in bed, especially in the winter, but I'd hear those footsteps on the other side of the house and knew exactly what that meant. Dad was up so I'd better get moving. We'd meet at the top of the stairs at around 4 a.m. Then we'd get into the car and take the twenty-minute or so trip from our house to work together. The two of us would ride in silence most of the way. The radio would be set to a sports or news station, not too loud. A typical conversation might revolve around the subject matter on the radio. I recall conversations such as:

"Those Yankees are really winning a lot of games lately, huh Dad?" I might say.

To which Dad would reply, "Shut up, don't talk so much!"

I could feel the love.

Upon arrival at our shop, we would continue our morning rituals and begin the workday. Days were long and hard but, in those days, we never had time to notice. The day would pass and, sometime between 6:30 and 7 p.m., we'd get in our car and head home. The ride home was usually a little more upbeat despite our exhaustion. We did this six days a week for many years. It was probably the most memorable time of our business for me.

As the years flew by, a lot changed. Our shop moved once, then again, and then one more time. Each time, Dad was there to offer guidance and assistance. His pen to paper attitude proved invaluable any time a big decision needed to be made. Analyzing the numbers and feasibility was as important as making a good sandwich, so he did just that. His signature negativity, though not always well received, has been an integral part of our continued success. After all, someone had to consider what can and may go wrong. His now famous "negative" quotations will be passed down from generation to generation. As we moved and struggled to keep the business going, we no longer traveled together. Somewhere along the line I had bought a house of my own. I recall the empty feeling of driving alone early in those first few years after I moved. I'd get to work and begin my day in complete solitude. There were no distractions, but the day never really got started until Dad arrived later in the morning and we shared a quick cup of coffee and brief conversation before the work day was officially under way.

Mornings are basically the same these days. I wake up early, around 4:45 a.m, and go to work. Life, however, is quite a bit different. I have a wife, a daughter, and three dogs. I have plenty more on my mind than I did when we started. The business, through ups and downs, is basically the same. It's still a sandwich shop, first and foremost. To get to work I drive roughly a half mile. It's a far cry from the days when Dad and I got into the car and drove together. I still spend the first few minutes getting started alone. Tasks have changed slightly, but I spend most of my time with food prep and customer service. Dad still maintains the books and offers advice, sometimes worthwhile advice, and sometimes not. Customers begin to arrive around 6:15. Some get drinks and others order egg sandwiches. Before that, usually around 5:45, while the shop is still quiet, a black car will slowly turn the corner into our parking lot. The door opens, and my dad will get out. Most days he'll toss a bag of trash from his house in the garbage bin. He then walks through the back door and greets me. Then, as he's done for so long, he puts on the day's first pot of coffee. He may be "Guapo" to the employees, but he'll always be Dad to me. That's still when my workday officially begins.

MEXICALI ROSE BURRITO

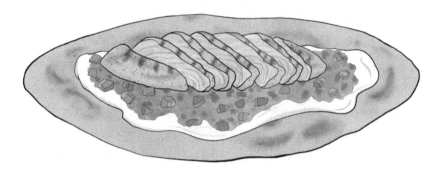

My dad and I entered this burrito in a contest years ago. Though it's one of our customers' favorites, we never found out if we won.

INGREDIENTS

4 12-inch plain wraps

4 thinly sliced chicken cutlets

3 eggs

1 cup seasoned bread crumbs

1 large chopped tomato

¼ pound sliced cheddar cheese

¼ pound sliced Monterey jack cheese

½ cup medium salsa (your favorite store brand will do)

½ cup sour cream

Olive oil

INSTRUCTIONS

Beat eggs in a small mixing bowl. Place cutlets in beaten eggs, then dredge each in bread crumbs, covering completely. Heat frying pan to medium and add enough olive oil to fry cutlets. Fry cutlets until golden brown on each side and internal temperature reaches 165 degrees.

Slice each cutlet into thin strips and place in mixing bowl. Add chopped tomatoes, sour cream and salsa and mix well.

Lay 12-inch wraps on a flat surface and layer slices of cheddar and Monterey jack cheeses. Add equal portions of chicken mixture to each wrap. Roll up and fold each wrap to form 4 neatly packed, stuffed burritos.

Reheat frying pan and cover bottom with olive oil. Place burritos in pan and cook lightly, rolling each as it browns slightly. When burritos are cooked all around, they are done. Pour an extra cup of salsa in case someone wants extra. Cutting in half is optional.

Plate and serve with Doritos Cool Ranch tortilla chips.

CHAPTER 23
TORAH, TORAH

I never thought I'd return to shul. After the age of thirteen and a serious shotgun bar mitzvah, I was unceremoniously shown the back door of the temple. Yes, I was dragged kicking and screaming to the bimah. The poor rabbi at my temple back then must have helped me recite half of the service. That's what happens when you don't memorize the Havtarah portion. Considering, up until then, my favorite part of religious school was recess and the football games the boys played, it was probably a good thing. So, it was a mutually beneficial separation. I didn't want to go to the temple and I'm fairly certain they didn't want me there.

That all changed about thirty years later. I had undergone some transformations since the age of thirteen: marriage, a daughter, and a lot less hair. A chance conversation with a customer would alter the course of my spiritual life.

A close friend of mine was initially just a walk-in customer of my sandwich shop a few years ago. He was a typical customer, sometimes breakfast, but mostly lunch. He fell, and still falls, into the category of customers who get the same sandwich day after day. He's the kind of customer that only needs to nod or motion with his hands to Santiago or me and we know exactly what he wants. (An interesting side note, he uses more napkins per meal than many small countries. It's his thing, but we don't hold it against him.) After he began frequenting our shop and became a regular, we began making small talk about wives, jobs, kids, etc., and a friendship grew. One day I asked him where his children attended school. With my daughter Lillian at the soon-to-be school age, I was beginning to worry about where she might go. He mentioned a Jewish day school, a private school located in the outskirts of Stamford. He and his wife loved the school, so he suggested we look into it. After a quick search I made an appointment with an admissions officer, Joanne. She did ask about our faith and indicated that, as a modern Orthodox school, they expected parents to be Jewish. I hesitated but played it as if I were fully aware of that expectation. I did not realize at the time what this would lead to for my family.

The day of our appointment came. Mei, Lillian, and I headed over to the school. We arrived, were greeted warmly and then led into an office where we would begin our introduction to the school. After a brief discussion and informative tour of the school that took most of the morning my wife and I agreed it would be the perfect place for our daughter. The staff was great, and the campus was just what you would expect from a private day school. Fortunately, we observed several classes in session that day. We could see just how dedicated the teachers were when Joanne led us from room to room. It was clear this school was our first choice for Lillian. The two of us were thrilled at the fact that we found a great school, and it was close to home. Although Lillian would not be attending for another year or so, it was nice to have one less thing to worry about. The only stumbling block, of course, was our complete lack of any religious background, other than my brief foray as a young boy. We had to rethink. The first thing we planned to do was find a temple.

Mei grew up as a spiritual, non-practicing Buddhist. Over the years we've known each other, on more than one occasion she's asked me to take her to a Jewish temple. "Temple is boring. Why would anyone want to go?" was my usual response. "When I was young I used to spend services counting lightbulbs and wondering when I could go home." She took my word for it year after year. Now, as parents, we were coming to a crossroad. It was time to think of our daughter and her future. With open minds and hearts, we decided to find a temple and see if the Jewish faith might welcome us. My wife made it clear that she would consider conversion, for her daughter.

She also made it clear that she would probably not convert for me, which made me feel warm all over! In my case, you never really stop being Jewish, you just stop going. Luckily, for us, we found a conservative temple in our city with a great rabbi willing to help. The chance conversation I'd had with my customer-turned-friend regarding school was beginning to develop into quite an experience.

The rabbi suggested we come to a Friday Shabbat service to experience it for ourselves. The last time I'd attended one of those was long ago. I was fully prepared to begin counting lights the night we decided to go for the first time. I think I even warned my wife in the car, "If it's really boring, I'm leaving early." The three of us arrived and were greeted with a typical Friday night greeting, "Shabbat Shalom." At first, I froze; I hadn't heard that in many years. I thought they might ask me the last time I was at temple, but they just seemed happy to see us. We found a seat and waited. About a hundred people were there that night. As I was anticipating the worst, something strange happened. The cantor, who leads services in song and prayer, began to sing. As a music lover I was shocked. The music was great, intoxicating. At one point I heard the familiar sounds of Leonard Cohen's music in the liturgy, the song "Hallelujah," one of my favorites. The cantor's voice was powerful, yet delightful and truly uplifting. By the end of the service my wife and I both felt spiritually moved. Our daughter, Lillian, on the other hand, did her best imitation of me as a child. She could not wait to leave, poor kid. This time I left with no idea how many lights were in the ceiling. We vowed to return.

After several more weeks of attending services and getting to know the rabbi it was decided. Mei would begin a conversion to Judaism and I would happily return to the Jewish faith. It seemed like they didn't mind having me and had forgotten all about my past. So much for the permanent records I'd heard about as a child. We loved the idea of having a faith-based family, so we began the process, and have truly enjoyed it every step of the way. Mei spent a year studying and learning under the tutelage of a very patient, supportive and didactic rabbi. I decided to study along with my wife, so we learned together. The only thing I could recall from my studies as a child was that the temple we belonged to had many, many lights! The learning process was educational and fun. With age comes wisdom. The rabbi really knew his stuff and was thrilled to have a couple of eager learners. We are grateful for his support and guidance. Believe it or not, even Lillian has enjoyed her time at temple. She has a good friend and actually looks forward to Friday services. She helps close the services singing a Hebrew song of peace on the bimah with her friend. It's adorable. At a young age, Lillian has embraced her religion as well as any child I know. This I never expected.

So, from a brief conversation with a friend, my family has come to the Jewish faith together. One day, to show my appreciation, I decided to take my napkin-abusing friend out for lunch. It was the least I could do. Naturally, we decided on a kosher deli not far from us. As we sat down and got ready to order I remember telling him that I never imagined being at shul on Friday nights. Of all the places in the city of Stamford, it was probably the last place I figured I'd be. He laughed it off and gave most of the credit to his wife. The waitress came over to take our order. I hadn't been to this particular kosher-style restaurant probably since I was around thirteen. I used to order corned beef. Though I've probably single-handedly boiled and served over a ton of corned beef for St. Patrick's Day year after year, I haven't eaten any since those childhood days. Since I was returning after a long hiatus, I might as well indulge. I ordered the largest pastrami and corned beef combo they had on the menu. I felt it was necessary to add pastrami. This sandwich is similar to one we offer at our shop, a very large triple-decker. Along with a cup of matzoh ball soup, it was the best kosher sandwich I'd had in a long time. Good to be back.

HUNGRY BEAR [21]

It's not exactly kosher, but it's been one of our most popular triple-deckers for years. We make it cold, but it can be served hot.

INGREDIENTS

12 slices of marble rye bread

1 pound lean corned beef

1 pound pastrami

¼ pound Swiss cheese

1 small head shredded green cabbage

1½ cups real mayonnaise

½ cup ketchup

¼ cup sweet relish

½ cup sour cream

¼ cup heavy cream

2 T sugar

1 T red vinegar

1 T caraway seeds

Salt and pepper

INSTRUCTIONS

To make Thousand Island dressing mix ½ cup mayo and ½ cup ketchup with sweet relish in mixing bowl. Put aside.

To make coleslaw place green cabbage in another mixing bowl. In food processor combine remaining cup of mayonnaise with sour cream, heavy cream, sugar, and red vinegar. Pour mixture over cabbage and add caraway seeds along with salt and pepper to taste.

Lay marble rye bread on flat surface. Spread Thousand Island dressing on one side of each slice. On four slices layer Swiss cheese, then equal amounts of corned beef. Place a slice of bread on top of each sandwich. Layer equal amounts of pastrami on all four sandwiches followed by generous amounts of coleslaw. Top off each with another slice of Swiss cheese and cover with remaining four slices of marble rye. Four triple-deckers! Cut in half and use toothpicks to keep each half intact.

Plate and serve with Lay's Harvest Cheddar SunChips.

CHAPTER 24
Now WHAT?

When this journey began way back in 1993 if you had told me I'd still be doing this over twenty-five years later I'd have said, "Five years, tops! Not a chance, no way I'll be behind the sandwich counter as I near fifty. Something else will come up." I'm still waiting for that something. Along with my wife I've thought long and hard, yet still am confronted with the same question. What else is out there? I used to say, "Just one more five-year lease option, then I'll reevaluate." Somehow five five-year options have gone by. It's even a topic of discussion between some of my customers and me. We marvel at the fact that they are still ordering lunch and I am still preparing it for them. Believe it or not, I've maintained some customers for twenty-five years now. Some of us have been through three decades together, going on four. In a world where loyalty is scarce, some of my best, and favorite, customers are the ones I've known since the early days. The questions that arise, now more than ever, are, How much longer do I have? How many more years will I own and operate the Gourmet Galley? How many more sandwiches can I make? There's a lot to consider.

The one major issue I have, as a result of years in the food service business, is pain. I never really expected that. My mom says getting old sucks! Nowhere is this more apparent than in my small business. The seven-day work weeks, the 60-, 70-, 80-hour weeks, are catching up with me. Waking up at 4:45 a.m. every day is getting a little old. Sure, it's fun for a few years, but try doing it for twenty-five-plus years. As a treat, I allow myself to sleep until 5:30 a.m. on weekends, but it doesn't help much. I suffer from carpal tunnel syndrome in both hands due to years of chopping, dicing and slicing.

My back hurts chronically from standing on hard, tile floors all day and my knees ache. The only advantage to my knee pain is that I can usually sense major weather changes in the air. People doubt me, but I bet I'm right almost as often as the local weatherman. In addition, pain in my right shoulder comes and goes like the breeze depending on the day. Yes, who would have ever guessed I'd be nursing chronic injuries due to many years of sandwich making? It's not like it's a contact sport. Nevertheless, I'm still not sure it's time to move on.

Making sandwiches is in my blood. It's some kind of genetic mutation that my mom passed down to me only. My sisters are not involved in the business or interested in making sandwiches for a living. It's just not clear what exactly keeps me motivated to arrive day after day, year after year to churn out lunch. Does it go back to that day in New York City when I first noticed the importance of lunch among the workers? Or does it go back even further, to when I first tasted the tantalizing flavors in an Italian combo? Or does it go back to my childhood, when the highlight of my Saturday was a big, tasty sandwich for lunch? I don't think I'll ever figure out why I have this genuine love for taking a few slices of bread and overstuffing them with meat, veggies and sandwich spreads to create complete lunch satisfaction. It really is my passion.

Moreover, there are numerous other reasons to continue "sandwiching" myself through the day. Looking back on the sandwiches in this book and the accompanying anecdotes, I can't help but feel nostalgia creep in a little. I know I can't do this forever, but how will the staff react? What will Santiago do without me? It's not fair to leave him to run the business alone. That's tantamount to torture! Also, will the sandwich machine simply shut down? Where will my dad go every morning? My well-meaning wife thinks it's time for me to move on. As helpful and supportive as she's been, she hasn't devoted her life as I have. She does not have the passion. My sandwich shop is my mistress. At least my wife knows I don't have the time, or the energy, for affairs. My daughter loves helping me at work, although actually, I think she likes eating the sandwiches more than helping. She proudly introduces me to friends by saying, "This is my dad. He makes sandwiches." (Perhaps one day she'll include "writes books" in that description, but I'll take it for now.) The close friends I've made, the fantastic customers I've been servicing all these years and the skills I've learned, these are the things, more often good than bad, that keep me from putting the top piece of bread on the sandwich of my life in the shop and saying goodbye to it all. Besides, I still get a somewhat maniacal degree of pleasure from loading up the walk-in cooler with stock at the beginning of the week and watching how it slowly, gradually empties out by Friday. The empty shelves mean one thing: lots of sandwiches the past week. Sure, the business itself has undergone changes over the years. Some I can do without, but there's still so much I love about sandwiching. Besides, I'm not trained to do anything else!

On the weekends my wife, daughter, and I usually go out shopping. Sometimes we go to a supermarket, while other times we might go to a home improvement center or department store. As we roam the aisles invariably I'll come across a familiar face. My fellow shopper will kind of look at me in a way that says they recognize me but aren't quite sure why. Out of context we all have a difficult time placing a face. A few seconds later the shopper will come to a realization and turn towards me. Following an awkward moment or two they might say, "Hey, you're that guy from the sandwich shop, in Stamford, right?" I'll smile and often tell them exactly what they ate the last time in my shop. "Yes I am, and you had a chicken cutlet, lettuce, tomatoes and mayo on a hero with jalapeños last time you came in!" After a quick laugh we shake hands and continue on our separate shopping paths. I might overhear them mention to their spouse or friend how my shop makes the best sandwiches in town. "That's the sandwich guy! I had an awesome lunch at Gourmet Galley last week, it really made my day!" he might say. As I walk away with my wife and daughter I wonder if I'm okay being known as the sandwich guy. I suppose there's a certain degree of pride associated with being known as something, even a sandwich maker. Yes, I think I'm okay with it . . . for at least a few more years. Maybe I've found that the secret for finding true happiness in life is buried somewhere in between two slices of bread.

ENJOY EVERY SANDWICH.
— WARREN ZEVON

ACKNOWLEDGMENTS

I would like to extend my sincere gratitude to family, staff, the greatest publishing team, and some of my best customers and friends. Without them this book would never have been written.

Family: First, my wife, Mei. Thank you for affording me the time to begin something we talked about for many years, and for convincing me to finish it. My mom, Phyllis, for being a business partner, proofreader, and devoted sandwich maker. My dad, Herb, whose signature negativity not only helped motivate me to write this book, but also, inadvertently, provided some of the most unforgettable one-liners in our history. Santiago, for everything he does . . . and it's a lot.

Staff: To all who have worked for Gourmet Galley over the years, the good, the bad and the unknown. You have all played an important role in our continued success.

Publishing Team: The first phase—Steven Himes, Telemachus Press, for your free advice and continued encouragement. Michael Balkind, author, for telling me to get started and setting me on my path to being an author. The second phase—Editor, Jeremy Townsend. Maybe the most important member of my publishing team. Your insight early on set the framework for the book and I'll be forever grateful for your input. Your editing services are second to none. Book designer, Barbara Aronica-Buck. I am very lucky to have found you through our temple. Your services were invaluable in setting up a great publishing team and in designing the final product. Book jacket designer, Lauren Harvey, for the perfect cover art. Proofreader, Kate Petrella. Thank you for the exceptional job you did with my book . . . so meticulous! Illustrator, Melanie B. Wong. Thank you for capturing the essence of this book wonderfully with your illustrations. Publicity services, Claire McKinney, of Claire McKinney PR. Thank you for your confidence and optimistic approach. You are the best in the business. Publisher, Plum Bay Publishing LLC, Mike Mulhern. Thank you for taking on this project and for having confidence in my work.

Customers and Friends: We've had so many great customers over the years that it would be impossible to list everyone. Neither the sandwich shop nor the book would have been feasible without the continued patronage of the great customers who have passed through our doors or have been loyal catering customers over the years. For that I thank every one of you. I've known some of you for so long I consider you not only customers, but friends. Thank you Maureen, Jude, Ann, Janine, Jackie, Kathy Jane and even Franceska. With customers like all of you, I just might continue making sandwiches for another 25 years!

ABOUT THE AUTHOR

Peter Roseman has spent his entire professional career, over 25 years, operating a sandwich shop, The Gourmet Galley, in lower Fairfield County. He spends his weekdays behind the deli counter serving up a wide variety of tasty sandwiches to his broad customer base at lunchtime. The past 25 years, the people, places and events related to his shop have been the inspiration behind *Sandwich'd*. Peter lives with his wife, Mei, daughter, Lillian, two dogs, Maggie and Beau, and a turtle named Tittles in Stamford, Connecticut, just a few blocks from his shop. When not at work, Peter likes to spend time with his family and loves to shop at local food stores in his never-ending search for new sandwich ideas and ingredients. If you are hungry, stop by his shop on Fairfield Avenue in Stamford, just a short drive off exit 6 on I-95.